PRAISES ABOUT FAMILY TAILS

"Beautiful memories of my own years as a mom washed over me as I read *Family Tails*. As I turned the pages, I found myself reliving my own life with my own children and enjoying them all over again. I remembered the sweetness, the simplicity, the tenderness, the tears, and the richness of those moments. Those "bits of happiness sprinkled through the days" when we lived life and soaked it up to the full.

"Each of the book's charming animal illustrations is a work of art that enhances the story, and the vivid descriptions of the flora and fauna of the author's garden world will appeal to the nature lovers who live nearby and those who wish they could visit Helena, Alabama to experience it themselves.

"This book will appeal to the young mom who hopes to see meaning in everyday moments of life with her children. It will warm the heart of the mother who is long past the days of having young ones at home, and it will remind her that those times were rich, poignant, and beautiful. It will appeal to those of us who have lived long enough to recognize the passing of an era where little boys grow up and neighborhoods change, and to remember the pets that joined us in the journey and taught us much about life.

"This is a book that I plan to read with delight and a warm cup of tea many times over."

—Jenny Wheeler, Teacher,
Mother of six, Grandmother of five

"The world is packed with sorrows and joys, great fears and wonderful peace, and for some lucky folks, enduring devotion and love. Deborah Elliott's beautiful memoir will bring a smile to your lips, perhaps a tear to your eye, and a sense that as we journey through this world of ours, we are fortunate to have our family and our animals accompany us.

"The true account of a family growing up in the small-town South, *Family Tails* includes a gamut of furry, scaled, and feathered friends: Susie, Shepherd, Miss Pepper, Autumn, and more dogs and cats, along with a squirrel, a lizard named Spot-Spike, an assortment of aquatic characters, and all the birds that inhabited the surrounding woods...and more! The mantra of the Elliott family was "We don't need another animal." The animals decided otherwise, and each and every animal brings new discoveries and emotions.

"This is a heartwarming, poignant, and inspiring story, and anyone who has ever had a one-sided conversation with a beloved dog or cat is sure to cherish it."

—Brad Strickland, PhD, Award winning author

"As time moves forward and things change, it is nice to look back at childhood and coming of age, especially when it is in the community we live in and love. In a time where everyone is looking to the future, it is nice to reminisce on days gone by. Reading about boys growing up in nature causes one to recall their own upbringing and boyhood adventures. As an animal lover, the tales of the timid creatures of the wild made me feel like I was right there beside them all."

—Brian Puckett, Mayor of Helena, Alabama

FAMILY TAILS

FAMILY TAILS

MY LIFE WITH BOYS, DOGS, AND OTHER AMAZING CRITTERS

DEBORAH H. ELLIOTT
ILLUSTRATED BY RON ADAIR

Goodroots Publishing

This is a true story. All events, characters, and conversations are portrayed as accurately as memory allows. Minor details may have been changed or added.

Published by: Goodroots Publishing

Hardcover ISBN: 979-8-9871238-0-5
Paperback ISBN: 979-8-9871238-1-2
eBook ISBN: 979-8-9871238-2-9

Cover and Interior Design: Creative Publishing Book Design
Cover Art and Interior Illustrations: Ron Adair

Printed in the United States of America

Dedicated to
Sam, Josh, and Mark,
And my dear husband Lou

CONTENTS

CHAPTER ONE

THE TREE HOUSE

I was the meanest mother in the world—my heart was hard and spitting out sparks like flint as I glared at the cute, squirming puppy in my husband's arms.

"Louis, where are we going to keep this animal? Have you forgotten we have white carpet?" (In reality the carpet was no longer white. It had acquired varying shades of tan and gray, and we had plans to replace it.) "I'm not taking care of an indoor dog," I declared. "I have just potty-trained two children, and now a dog? No way! If we're going to have a dog, we need a place with a fence and a yard to keep it in."

Lou stood inside the front door and looked at me sadly as I scolded him. The puppy turned its luminous brown, beseeching eyes toward me.

1

"And besides all that, Lou, you know that Josh has problems with asthma. An indoor dog will make his breathing worse."

My husband hung his head, for he had no argument against the health of his child.

Lou and I had started our family in a tree house. It was a relatively conventional cedar and brick abode, but the setting was exceptional. We could touch the tops of dogwood trees from its wraparound deck, and in the distance we could see the slopes of Double Oak Mountain, a verdant ridge that is part of the southwestern-most tip of the Appalachian range stretching into central Alabama. The house had wide stretches of glass to take advantage of the sylvan views, and cooling breezes flowed through the windows along with birdsong and the chatter of squirrels. Crowded buildings and busy highways and harsh city sounds did not disturb our peace, and it was easy to imagine ourselves truly perched amidst the tree tops.

But it wasn't a good place for children. Lou and I didn't know this when we bought it. We weren't parents yet, and we were ignorant about a lot of things.

I am embarrassed to recall that once, while I was still expecting my first child, I announced to a coworker, "I'm going to be an excellent parent."

Her eyebrows shot up when I said that. She already had children of her own. "You are?"

"Sure. I've read all these books, and I think I'll be good at it."

At that moment God must have gazed over me, shaken his head, and laughed out loud.

By the time we were house-hunting in 1979, we had been married for four years and had settled into the mainstream of life. Lou had a job as a pharmaceutical sales rep, while I worked as a staff nurse at University

Hospital in metropolitan Birmingham. When we were newly wed, Lou and I had determined to live on his salary alone and to put the money I made into savings. The years of frugal economics had paid off, and after years of apartment living we were at last on the brink of the good life. We bought our first house and planned for a baby.

We were nature lovers, and the tree house, nestled into the bosom of a forest, appealed to all our senses. I remember the first time we toured the house with the realtor. Homes in the area were tucked into land lush with vegetation—oak, pine, holly, hickory, cedar, and dogwood; forsythia, hydrangea, magnolia, and azalea. We stood on a hill, listening to the birds serenade us and breathing in the woodsy smells of earth and forest. We gazed up the monstrously steep, curving concrete driveway to a house above us that clung to the deep green, leafy terrain. A bit of sloping Zoysia lawn in front of the house bordered a small flat clearing that was sprinkled with pine straw. Otherwise, the property consisted of mountainous, wild woodland. The land rose sharply to the far right of the structure, and as we searched through the foliage on that end, we caught a glimpse of a house near the top of the ridge. An enormous brick retaining wall held up the left side of the driveway in front of us, preventing the whole thing from sliding down on top of the other neighbor at the bottom of the hill. A mailbox was located at the foot of the driveway, so retrieving the mail promised a good daily cardiovascular workout. A tiny warning tried to break through to our consciousness.

"It doesn't have much of a yard for children," Lou commented.

We briefly considered this, but emotions have a way of camouflaging the facts. We had already fallen in love with the greenery. The windows of our current apartment faced an eroding red clay bank, and we both longed for trees.

3

"True. But kids grow up on hillsides all over the world. Just look at the deck. It wraps all the way around the house. And the screened porch is wonderful. There's plenty of room for a child to play."

We noted the white carpet in the bedrooms when we went inside the house, but we were so ignorant we didn't even discuss that.

The year after we bought the tree house, we had our first child, a little boy we named Sam. His brother Josh arrived sixteen months later. Having armed myself with volumes of childrearing information, I embraced my role of parent with gusto. I left my hospital job and began teaching childbirth classes a couple evenings a week. This allowed me to be a full-time mommy during the day. We had an ordinary life. It was a common and good existence—the American dream.

Soon after Sam and Josh were born, we discovered that children do not need a big wraparound deck to play upon. They need dirt. You can do all sorts of things with dirt. You can dig in it. You can plant things in it and pull things out of it. You can create amazing make-believe worlds with it. You can find creepy little critters in it. You can mix it with water and get really messy. And you can bring it into the house with you and dump it all over the white carpet.

With a deck you get splinters.

We were fortunate to have good neighbors. Across the street lived the Satterwhites. They had three teenage daughters who were first-rate baby sitters. This was a huge advantage to our location that was not advertised in the real estate listings, but one we came to appreciate after we had children.

Next door to the Satterwhites lived the Pates, a family with four children. Their youngest daughter, Caroline, who was about age nine at the time, was our neighborhood's ambassador. She knew everybody on the street and came by regularly to keep me informed on all the local gossip and to chat about what various families were eating for supper.

"I have to go," Caroline told me one day as she was concluding her visit. "I need to see Omar before I go home." Omar was an infant whose parents had recently emigrated from Poland. The father was some sort of engineer, though there was a hushed-up rumor that he was a former spy in the witness protection program. Deep in the heart of Alabama was probably a good place for a spy to hide, if that were true.

"Omar? How are you going to talk to them?" I asked. Omar's mother did not speak English, and, as far as I knew, Caroline did not speak Polish.

"Oh, no problem!" Caroline confidently answered.

"Be careful on that driveway!" I called after her as she hopped down my front steps. She turned and waved, flashing a big smile.

The Millsaps occupied the house below us. They were an older couple, nearing retirement age, whose adult daughter Jane lived with them. She had been born with a syndrome that caused mental retardation and obesity, and she weighed well over three hundred pounds. Once when I was complaining about something my two-year-old was doing, Mrs. Millsap chuckled and said she knew just what I meant. I was sobered by the thought that Jane was perpetually two, and I marveled at her mother's strong and cheerful spirit. Years later I came to understand that mighty souls are tempered within the crucible of hardship.

The Millsaps watched over me when Lou was out of town on business trips. The roads were impassable after a rare ice storm in April one year. Lou was stuck in Huntsville in north Alabama and wasn't able to get home for a couple of days. A sheet of ice covered our driveway, trapping the boys and me up on our hillside. The phone rang, and it was Mrs. Millsap.

"You have a long rope, don't you? You do? Well, get out here and drop it over the wall. I have your supper for you, if you can pull it up."

I found the rope, put on my coat, gloves, and hiking shoes, and then went outside. The storm was gone, leaving behind a sunny, brilliant blue sky. I squinted at the bright light. Warm spring air would return in a few days, but now a gust of cold, sharp wind stung my face. Frosty white puffs came from my mouth with each breath. The last vapors of winter had deposited swaths of ice over homes, trees, and vehicles. Pine limbs crackled and bent under the weight of icicles, and a shivery layer of frost covered the grass. I thought of an image of Old Man Winter stooped over with a bad case of arthritis, leaning on his cane as he stood in the frozen woodlands. I cautiously made my way across the slippery drive to the brick ledge that bordered the driveway. I peered over the edge. Mrs. Millsap was waiting at the bottom of the retaining wall.

"Nice day, isn't it?" she called up to me, smiling.

"Why, yes, it is." I took a deep breath and looked around again to admire the scene as sunlight sparked throughout the ice-encrusted landscape, transforming wood and leaf and grass and ground into bejeweled wonderland.

I dropped one end of the rope over the retaining wall. Fifteen feet below me, Mrs. Millsap grabbed it. She tied it securely to a big pot of hot chicken soup, and I pulled it up. That night the boys and I gave thanks for good food and caring neighbors. A few weeks later, when Caroline told me the Millsaps all had come down with bad colds, I returned the favor by preparing some chicken soup and taking it to them. I was a little nervous about how my own recipe would compare to Mrs. Millsap's delicious version.

Afterwards, her hearty thanks reassured me. "Now, that chicken soup tasted like the chicken flew in it, rather than over it."

Mrs. Millsap was a compassionate soul, and she extended her generous care to both humans and animals. Our wooded neighborhood teemed with creatures of all sorts, and we soon discovered that, like us, the Millsaps appreciated their presence.

People caught up in the rush of daily living too often isolate themselves from the animal kingdom, rarely pausing to think about life outside the human community and unconcerned about what happens to wild lives. They lock themselves inside brick, wood, and concrete buildings and come out only to jump into vehicles in order to hurry off to other brick, wood, and concrete buildings. Uninformed by encounters with the natural world, parts of their lives remain incomplete, void of content and purpose. They also are missing out on some good entertainment.

One evening not long after we had moved to the tree house, I was rattling around in the kitchen, cleaning up some dishes, when a face outside the window startled me. I sucked in my breath.

"What! What is that thing? Lou, come here and look at this animal. It's sitting in the dogwood tree, and it's staring at me through the window. It looks like a giant rat!"

Lou came to investigate. The voyeur was an unlovely thing, with a long naked, pink tail and big beady eyes. "Oh, that's a possum. He must be hungry."

"Gee, I don't think I've ever seen a living possum before. I've only seen them squashed on the side of the road."

In fact, I had seen too many dead ones. Opossums are slow-moving nocturnal creatures and often end up as unfortunate road kill under the wheels of trucks and cars, for they have a dangerous tendency to stop in the street and stare stupidly at oncoming lights. As unappealing as their appearance may be, omnivorous opossums are good for the environment, eating such things as carrion, cockroaches, poisonous snakes, ticks, and rats. But they also can appreciate a good steak.

I opened the kitchen's sliding glass door and tossed some leftover ribeye scraps onto the platform feeder we kept for the birds. The possum dropped from the tree branch to the deck railing and waddled toward the food. Pleased with the fine dining, it became a regular visitor after that night, with a habit of glaring at me through the window while it perched in the dogwood tree and waited for its goodies. On a dark night, sometimes all I could see were its round, glow-in-the-dark eyes, seemingly disembodied, peering out of the darkness.

"Mrs. Millsap, you won't believe who has been coming by for supper every night," I said to my neighbor several weeks later.

"Who, or what, would that be?"

"A big possum. You ought to see him. He'll eat anything, but he loves steak scraps."

"Steak scraps, huh? Well, no wonder he's so fat. We've been feeding that critter, too, but we've never given him steak scraps."

"What? You've been feeding him, too?"

"Every night."

We named the possum Oscar, until one evening it showed up with a trimmer figure and with a bunch of babies clinging to its belly. We renamed her Oscaretta.

We usually kept the feeder on the deck filled with birdseed. Mockingbirds, sparrows, thrushes, wrens, blue-jays, and chickadees were fun to watch and a delight to listen to, but my favorite was a male cardinal who, with his black mask and brilliant red plumage, reminded me of a dandy dressed for the queen's masquerade ball. He was a bold character, tapping on the kitchen window with his beak when the feeder was empty, then flying to a nearby branch to watch me fill it. He would cock his head and cheep at me. I was never sure whether he was thanking me or telling me to hurry it up.

Cardinals are monogamous and mate for life. I admired how our male cardinal would affectionately bring seeds to his wife. He would carefully transfer the food to her. Beak to beak, the birds looked as if they were kissing. The couple often sang to each other, and I enjoyed listening to their duets.

Unlike her partner, the female was shy of humans. She watched carefully from the woods and joined her mate at the feeder only when Lou and I were off the deck. Even then, she kept an eye on the surroundings while she ate her fill. But the two of them brought their babies to the bird feeder after the young ones were old enough to leave the nest. Lou and I smiled at the little birds hopping about the deck right outside our kitchen's big glass door. Ever since, there has been a special place in my heart for cardinals.

The squirrels, however, were the ones who greedily gobbled most of the birdseed. We didn't realize how much our feeder had become part of their daily routine until a couple years after we moved in, when we had the deck across the back of the house rebuilt. The morning after the carpenters had torn off the old decking, we awakened to a cacophony of wild shrieking coming from the woods. We looked out the window expecting to witness the bloody carnage of some ferocious battle, only to discover that the squirrels were engaging in a group tantrum, furious that their feeder was gone. We made sure that the rebuilt deck held a new, improved feeder.

True to their heritage, my children were fascinated by the wildlife that dwelt in the forest around us. One day when he was fifteen months old and barely beginning to put words together, I cautioned Sam to be careful of a dead bee that was lying on the deck. He bent over and considered the insect. It must have impressed him, for the next day he pointed at a small piece of black, fuzzy yarn stuck to the living room couch and came out with an astonishing full sentence: "Hey, Mama, he a dead bee."

I gave Sam a book about common household pests when he was two years old, and he spent hours studying its colorful pictures of insects. He often caught lizards and bugs (a foreshadowing of bigger and better things to come). He had a small critter cage and some glass jars for the purpose. I told him these creatures could visit for a while—a few hours or maybe a day—but then they had to go home to the woods. Little green anole lizards occasionally found their way into the house, and I would spy them shimmying up the wall or across the floor. I could always count on quick-handed Sam to catch them for me.

In those days the children and I often visited the Birmingham Zoo, the city's Botanical Gardens, and all the neighborhood parks within easy driving distance. Many mornings I would pack our lunch, then load the double-stroller into the trunk of my Chevy Nova. That double stroller was an expensive item that paid for itself many times over. Lightweight and easily collapsible, it fit neatly into my car's trunk. I used it until both boys had outgrown it and its seams were coming apart. After buckling the boys into their car seats, I would carefully back the car down the curving driveway and then head out for a day of exploration, not to return until late afternoon.

We rarely were in a hurry. We soaked up life. We smelled it. We tasted it. We grabbed hold of it and ran with it. Or we just sat and observed it. One of the delights of having children was seeing the world again through the impressionable eyes of childhood. Every thing, great or small, was a curiosity to be examined or a treasure to share.

One morning at a neighborhood park, Sam and Josh noticed some turtles that were snoozing in the sunshine on a log in the middle of a small pond. My sons squatted beside the water and studied each terrapin. They admired the yellow stripes on their faces and the patterns of their hard shells. Then they grew quiet and waited steadfastly as they eyed the turtles, the minutes dragging by with the world paused in expectation. Suddenly, the boys whooped and danced when one of the turtles slid off the log and splashed into the water.

I considered my children. They were adorable. Sam was slender, with dark brown eyes and a mass of golden-brown ringlets that sparkled in the sunlight and bounced whenever he moved his head. Fair-skinned Josh was plump, and he had a thicket of almost-straight, white hair and big gray-blue eyes. My boys were so different from each other. Someone who did not know us would not imagine them to be kinfolk, much less brothers. People would stare at them in the double stroller, Josh in the front with Sam behind him. Looking at me with my own dark eyes and brown hair, they would point to Sam.

"Now this one is yours. Is the other one his friend?"

"Oh, no," I would assure them. "They are both mine. Same daddy. Same genetic pool. Isn't it great?"

Soft, squeezable Josh was serene and contemplative, with the soul of a future artist and musician. Sam was a wiry wild man, sharp-minded, an explorer. Sam was a trip to an amusement park, full of fun and scary thrills. Josh was a walk through a quiet, sun-dappled forest. Both were wonderful experiences, and having them both was best of all.

I smiled as they lay on their bellies with their heads together, pointing at tiny fishes. They squealed when a blue dragonfly with huge globular eyes and long gossamer wings landed nearby. The sun was pleasantly warm. It was a gentle, lazy day, as I sat watching my children watching the water. I could have been bored except for the joy of discovery I could see in their shining faces.

This is one thing my children taught me when they were very young: the good stuff comes in moments, bits of happiness sprinkled through the days, more so than in the great events that are spaced apart through the years. If we never linger to appreciate the subtle pleasures that rest in the common spaces of our daily lives, how many of life's blessings do we leave behind, overrun by work and worries?

We purchased a family membership to the Birmingham Zoo so we could visit as often as we wanted. It was always a source of interesting experiences—and sometimes not what we expected. One particular day we entered the gates and walked down the path toward the alligators. These large reptiles usually spent their time resting quietly in their enclosure, either in their shallow pond or upon its grassy banks. On this day, however, we halted, shocked, when the alligators came into sight.

Gaping wounds covered their bodies. Blood oozed between fractured scales. Apparently there had been a savage free-for-all. A couple of the reptiles were still snarling, showing their nasty teeth to the onlookers. A zoo keeper, who was a brave fellow for sure, was catching them with a long pole with a loop on the end of it, which he skillfully used to keep their menacing jaws shut. We stood for over an hour and gawked as the zoo veterinarian tranquilized and stitched up each alligator. It was a gory sight to rival any nature show on television. Sam and Josh, male beings to the core, loved it.

Another memorable day at the zoo began with a visit to see the noble cats. Most of them were resting in the shade of some large boulders inside the large, naturalized exhibit, but a couple of the big cats were pacing. They looked sleek and dangerous as they padded back and forth, sometimes eyeing the spectators. Next we watched the primates on monkey island, the young ones swinging on ropes and leaping from rock to rock, while their elders sat preening and grooming each other's fur. After admiring the monkeys, we walked over to see the polar bears, so out of place in the Deep South that in the heat of summer their keeper brought in great piles of ice to create a cool retreat for them. One bear, a natural ham accustomed to the crowds, stood up and waved at us. The three of us waved back. Then we moved on to see our favorites, the sea lions. They barked and splashed in the aquamarine water of their swimming pool. They reminded me of frolicking children who were enjoying a refreshing dip. Having worked up a sweat ourselves, we wished we could join them.

By then it was time for the concession stands. I hadn't brought any sandwiches with us that day—a pricey mistake—so I bought drinks and hot dogs, and we settled at a picnic table to eat. We had barely begun our meal when a peacock approached. Josh held his hot dog about midway to his mouth as he paused to admire the jewel-colored bird with its iridescent body of cobalt-blue and its rich jade, copper, and turquoise tail feathers. In a flash, the greedy fowl grabbed the hot dog and gulped it down. Josh and Sam hooted at the bird's audacity, but I grumbled as I forked over more money to buy another hot dog.

After lunch we strolled over to the elephants and noted a pair of huge beasts. They had enormous heads and long trunks. Their dusty, grayish-brown, wrinkled skin had patches of scrubby, coarse hair. It was a typical Alabama summer day, and we were perspiring as we watched them. The massive animals knew how to keep themselves comfortable in the heat. They adroitly used their wide, flat ears as fans to cool themselves, and they kept flies away by gently swishing their tails side to side. But what fascinated us most was how they swept up dirt with their trunks, then sprayed it across their backs—apparently dirt makes a good natural sunscreen.

I looked at the elephants' enclosure. It was maybe a thousand square feet—not much space for two large elephants. It was sad. The elephants were safe and well-nourished, but I wondered if they would have been happier in the wild, along with most of the other zoo animals.

Yet I was glad my sons could see these wonderful creatures. Zoos engage in scientific research, and they play an important role in educating the public and in promoting conservation of animal species. Many animal populations are under severe threat of extinction in the wild due to loss of habitat, overhunting and poaching, environmental changes, and other factors. Many times the decline in animal populations is caused directly or indirectly by man, sometimes in malice, often in ignorance. Education is a fundamental part of wildlife protection.

In the late 1990's, the Birmingham Zoo lost its accreditation by the Association of Zoos and Aquariums, largely because of the poor facilities it provided for their elephants. But the zoo has come many miles since those times. Now the Birmingham Zoo is accredited by the AZA and is a participant in the AZA Species Survival Plan Program. Recognized for their role in the care and conservation of elephants, today the zoo features "Trails of Africa," a fourteen-acre exhibit with natural habitat for elephants and other animal species native to Africa's savannah.

After watching the elephants, we walked next door to the hippo-potamus house. The light inside was dim, and the air was humid and had the strong smell of animal poop. I held Josh, and Sam stood beside me as we leaned against the railing and tried to see down into the pit where some creatures were lolling around under the water. As our eyes adjusted, we could make out a couple of brown humps and some giant hairy nostrils breaking the surface of the murky water. We were about to move on when the water directly below us began to stir, and an enormous head erupted out of the depths and water slid off a hippo's corpulent backside. The behemoth opened its mouth wide, and for a startling moment we stared into its pink interior, past the long sharp incisors in front and the big flat molars in back, down toward its tonsils, until suddenly the mouth smacked shut and the head and body slammed back into the pool. The roiling water rose up and rained down over us. We shrieked and backed away. Our clothes were soaked with the fetid pool water, and we carried a certain hippo house aroma with us the rest of the afternoon. Nevertheless, we were out to have an adventure, and since adventurers lap up new experiences like ice cream on a hot summer's day, we all agreed the visit to the zoo was a success.

Frequent outings allowed the children to jump and shout and play hard. This was essential, considering the dangerous topography of our own yard. After a long day of recreation, we would return to the house. The boys would be tuckered out, ready for supper, bath, and bed. By seven-thirty they were asleep. The remainder of the evening was free for the adults to enjoy, and as an additional bonus, the house was still relatively clean, because we hadn't been there all day to destroy it.

I said "relatively" clean, because mess-making is an ongoing process with small children. Wherever my children went, they left a little debris field behind them. When we were expecting special guests and wanted the house to look nice, Lou would take the boys out for several hours while I stayed home to mop, vacuum, and put away toys—and to wipe sticky little fingerprints from all those big windows. We had to time this right so that Lou would come back with the children just prior to the arrival of our guests. People sometimes commented on how clean I kept the house. If only they knew.

Lou inherently liked everything to be tidy. Once while we were still dating, he came to visit me in my apartment, which I shared with my friend Dee from college. She had been sewing, and a pile of fabric scraps and dress patterns lay in a corner by the sewing machine. Lou looked at the disorder with disapproval.

"When we get married, we won't have messes like that in our house," he said.

Oh, yeah. Right. Children will change you, and I can truthfully testify that my husband and his boys made some marvelous messes together with mountains of building blocks, miles of race car and train tracks, and piles of camping equipment scattered throughout the house.

Sam liked to take the house apart. Literally. He was very good with a screwdriver. He disassembled toys, lamps, and furniture. We rarely were able to reassemble these things, because he usually dropped some pieces down the air vents in the floors, whereby they fell deep into the unreachable bowels of the house. Someday, when that house is torn down, somebody is going to find a pile of treasure from the early 1980's, including spoons and forks, small action figures from McDonald's Happy Meals, screws, bolts, nuts, and all sorts of plastic and metal parts. When he was two years old, I caught Sam taking apart the brass bed, working patiently with a screwdriver. Fortunately, none of the important pieces had yet found their way to the air vents.

He was also fond of plumbing. Despite my best efforts at discipline, Sam continually took the toilet tank lid off and disconnected a hose in there that made a terrific water gun. I marveled that he never dropped the heavy tank lid or hurt himself while lifting it. He sprayed the bathroom walls so many times that the wallpaper peeled off.

This hyperactive child also determined that anything that was on a shelf needed to be on the floor. "Why are you doing this?" I asked one morning when I caught him sweeping magazines off a table.

"Because I have to," was his honest reply.

There was no shelf beyond his reach, because he was an excellent climber. When he was twelve months old, he climbed to the top of a five foot stepladder. When he was fifteen months old, I came into the dining room just as he was standing on top of the table, stretching his arms upward with intent to grab the chandelier for a good Tarzan swing. I was worn out watching over him. I sometimes found him balanced on the window sill with his body pressed against the glass, staring outward, like a small caged bird that wanted to fly free.

Sam needed SPACE.

We managed. We adapted to our home's limitations, and we visited places and did fun things that we might never have done if we had lived on flatter land. Sam and Josh were forbidden to play on our driveway. Riding toys on that steep, curving driveway had a good chance of landing on the Millsap's roof. When other preschoolers were learning to ride tricycles, Lou tied ropes around my boys' waists and taught them to rappel down the backyard.

We owned no pets, except for Lou's tank of tropical fish, but sometimes neighboring animals dropped by to visit. A beautiful English springer spaniel named Hunter lived up the road. He liked our front yard. He would lie on his back with all four legs stuck up in the air, and working his hips like a belly dancer, he would slide down the sloping patch of Zoysia grass, then hop up and lope to the top of the hill to do it all over again. Hunter was a friendly, playful dog. The only bad thing he ever did was to steal Josh's shoe right off his foot, then run home with it. We loved Hunter.

Sam and Josh wanted a dog of their own, but we did not have the right yard for one. I truly felt terrible the day Lou came through the front door with a puppy in his arms, but it was the voice of reason that hardened my heart and demanded he take it back.

The sad thing is that, like dirt, children need doggies.

We continued to live in the tree house, despite its limitations, because we loved its big windows and spacious, airy rooms and its incredible natural surroundings. And we loved our neighbors. How could we leave?

Sometime after the puppy incident, local news reports filled up with the exciting possibility of snow. There were wild speculations about the need to close roads and schools. People rushed out to grocery stores to buy milk and bread and last minute emergency items such as batteries. It is a Deep South ritual. Without snowplows or other snow equipment, Alabama essentially shuts down if there is any amount of frozen precipitation. For a lot of people, snow signals an unexpected holiday. Josh was three and Sam was four, and they had never experienced snow. They had seen it in books. They had seen it on television. It was something that happened in faraway frozen places, but not in our front yard. Now they climbed up on the sofa and pushed their faces against the big window as the gray sky filled up with magic crystals swirling down from another world. Their eyes widened as garlands of icy jewels settled upon the trees and sparkling white powder covered the ground. It was the stuff of fairy tales and Santa's homeland.

Some grown-ups complain about slippery walkways and hazardous driving conditions, but in our part of the country even many adults are children at heart when it comes to snow. And for a child, snow means one thing:

"Let's build a snowman!"

Children in places like New York and Minnesota can take their snowmen for granted. They can build their snowmen, knock them down, then build some more. In central Alabama, building a snowman is a rare and special occasion. An Alabamian may get to build only one or two good snowmen during an entire childhood. I still remember the three big ones my two brothers and I built after a huge snowfall on New Years Eve when I was twelve years old.

This particular snowman that my sons built would send our family around a turning point that we could have predicted but did not really see coming.

We didn't get much snow, maybe half an inch. It was just enough to coat the grass and to bead the pine trees and to close the roads and to shut down the schools, but hardly enough to make a decent snowman. In spite of this, Lou bundled the boys up in warm coats, hats, and mittens, and out the three of them went. I stayed inside to prepare soup and hot chocolate.

I watched through the window while they worked. It was an endearing scene. They labored up and down the slanting ground, gathering up snow until they had scraped almost all the white powder off our patch of front lawn, packing it and then molding it into two large balls. The boys laughed, and their pink faces shone as they balanced one ball on top of the other to make a body. They found sticks for arms, gave it a face with pieces of charcoal, and placed a hat on its head. After they finished, they stood back to admire their genuine snowman.

And then that snowman rolled down the hill and splattered into a gazillion pieces.

Sam and Josh came into the house, their little bodies racked by sobs and long, shuddering breaths. Lou followed them inside. He was grim.

He looked me in the eye and announced, "We are moving."

CHAPTER TWO

Susie

Five months after the snowman catastrophe, we had found a new home in Helena, a small town about twenty miles south of Birmingham. We sold the tree house to a single woman who had no children and said goodbye to our neighbors, though this was not as wrenching as it might have been. The Millsaps had recently moved, the Pates were also gone, and the Satterwhites had begun their own search for a new house. Our mountainside was a neighborhood in flux. We emptied the tree house of all our accumulated junk and jammed it into a moving van. The volume of our possessions amazed me. How could we have acquired so much stuff in only five years?

Before we began our house search, I had never heard of Helena, but I soon learned that it has an interesting history for such a small place. Back during the Civil War, the community was known as Hillsboro, and it operated a top-secret rolling mill to produce materials for the Confederate Army. It was a productive plant until 1865, when the Yankees came through and burned the place to the ground. After the war, the L&N Railroad sent an engineer named Pete Boyle to build a train station, and, being a romantic guy, he called it "Helena Station," after his sweetheart. The surrounding land began to develop, and the city was incorporated in 1877. The steel mill reopened, and several coal mines, a grist mill, and a large railroad yard contributed to the local economy. A cotton gin opened next to the train station.

Helena prospered for years, but after the steel mill and the coal mines closed in the 1920's, the town went into decline. In 1933, a devastating tornado depressed the area further, and Helena spent most of the twentieth century outside the fast-paced currents of progress. For many years there was one police officer, a tiny jail to accommodate the occasional drunk, and a volunteer fire department. Trains blew forlorn whistles as they passed through on tracks that crisscrossed the town's borders. The population numbered in the hundreds, and farmland surrounded the town hall and the few other buildings on Main Street.

But by the time we moved to Helena in 1985, the town was on the cusp of modernization and explosive growth. Its population had grown to several thousand people, though it still had folksy charm and a post office that rarely had a waiting line, even during the rush of Christmas season. There were no traffic lights in the community, only stop signs.

The old, one-level house we bought wasn't pretty, but it did have promise. It had peeling green paint, a flat roof, and a long overhang across the center that made the structure look like a trailer with an eyebrow. Inside were thick wooden beams and heart pine paneling that had been milled years ago from trees cut from the property. It had spacious rooms, plenty of big windows, durable wooden floors, and two working fireplaces, including one in the kitchen. What greater luxury could a woman ask for? There was a private office for Lou, and there was a parking area behind the house big enough for a fleet of cars (In the back of our minds, though we didn't want to think much about it, was the knowledge that our boys would eventually turn into teenagers with drivers' licenses).

Best of all, our new residence was located within three-and-a-half acres of private, gently rolling land at the end of a scenic drive. Towering oaks and a forest of mature dogwood trees encircled a nice lawn, and a large fenced-in area would make a perfect dog yard. There was a field for playing ball and a wild valley to explore. Children could run and ride bikes and dig in the dirt and have a puppy—as well as other assorted creatures I never dreamed of bringing into my household. We moved in June 1985, and the sturdy house opened its doors and welcomed us home.

After we had been in Helena about six weeks, we had arranged the furniture and hung a few pictures. We had assigned dishes, clothing, and toys to appropriate locations in hopes they might actually be put there on occasion. We had piled a mountain of empty cardboard boxes outside to await garbage pick-up, which at the time depended on a guy who would come by to collect trash in his pick-up truck. The same man was a jack-of-all-trades who also performed other assorted jobs for the city.

Now the top priority was to get a dog. We were somewhat snobbish. This would be no mutt picked up on a whim. We developed a list of criteria for the animal. It must 1) have a gentle temperament, 2) have a strong constitution bred for outdoor living, and 3) be intelligent. Lou talked to a friend who recommended we get an English setter. So one weekend we loaded Sam and Josh into the car and drove to Smokerise, a community north of Birmingham, to see some English setter puppies advertised in the newspaper.

We parked in front of a wide lawn sprinkled with clover, dandelion, and other assorted weeds and wildflowers. A graying middle-aged man came out of a brick house and greeted us. He showed us to a generous fenced-in area beside the house. The sky was overcast, and the ground was still wet from recent rain. Some large doghouses occupied one side of the enclosure, and several adult dogs and a couple of puppies roamed the area.

"We have two pups left, one male and one female. The one with brown spots is the male, black spots is the female."

He opened the gate, and we walked in. The brown and white male puppy was near the gate and greeted us first. He calmly sat and accepted our praises and petting. He was sweet. The female, who had black spots sprinkled over her body and a great black patch covering one eye, was romping on the other side of the yard, poking her nose into everything, dancing around her discoveries. When she saw us, she came up to our boys with wagging tail, wiggling body, and an invitation to play. She captured our hearts immediately. Oh yes, she would fit right into our family.

The owner picked her up and turned her onto her back. She squirmed in his arms a moment, then quieted and stared up at us with soulful eyes.

"This is a fine animal," the owner said. "She's got great form, and she shows real hunting talent. I don't know. I was thinking about keeping her and training her for myself."

The man was eyeing us, no doubt sizing up our pocketbook as he recited her championship bloodline, describing the lofty accomplishments of her parents and grandparents. "This dog is bound for good things, I would predict."

"Well, all that sounds great, but really we were just looking for a pet."

He gawked at us like we were bona fide nuts. "Pet? I've never sold one of these dogs as a pet."

However, despite the obvious loss to the hunting world, he was happy to sell her, and soon we were traveling homeward with the black and white puppy.

"What shall we name her?" I asked Sam and Josh.

"Black-eyed Susan because of the patch over her eye." This suggestion came from Sam.

Black-eyed Susan is also the name of the yellow, daisy-like flowers with black centers that bloomed in mass on the bank beside our driveway.

"Why, Sam," I said, "did you know that Black-eyed Susans usually grow wild in fields, and English setters are field dogs. I think that would be a perfect name."

The problem is, you can't easily holler "Black-eyed Susan!" out the kitchen door, so she quickly became Susie.

I was concerned about how the puppy would adjust to her new home after being so abruptly taken from her mother and brother. But within minutes after we arrived home, Susie was playing with Sam and Josh, chasing after big pine cones they tossed and then running back to the boys and jumping into their laps. Now we were her family.

Toward humans, Susie was a gentle dog. I once put her to the test by taking a piece of meat out of her mouth after she had begun to chew on it. This is not a test recommended by dog training manuals. In this case, Susie didn't even growl, although the dirty look she gave me let me know how she felt about the matter. She would never bite a child.

But under her sweet exterior beat the heart of a predator.

The morning after we brought her home, we let her out of the spacious fenced-in dog yard to play with us. As she came loping around the corner of the house, she saw several doves resting on the front lawn. She slammed to a stop, and her whole body shuddered as if a genetic switch had flipped and a jolt of electricity had passed through her. Then, powered by the blood of champions, she charged forth after the birds with the passion of destiny.

We never trained her, but soon she instinctively was coming to point, with her tail straight and stiff and front paw raised as she detected her prey. She was Super Dog. Nothing could escape her penetrating senses—with her keen vision and nose she could identify creatures hidden behind trees and under bushes.

As she zeroed in on her target, she would stand stock-still, except for a slight quiver of her rear end that gave evidence to mounting tension. Then, like a canine heat-seeking missile, she would launch herself toward her quarry, and the chase would begin. The seller was right. She would have been a great hunting dog.

I come from a family of animal lovers. My mother was the kind of person who prepared special meals for her pets. My oldest brother Mike told me about the day he entered her house and smelled the delicious aroma of chicken cooking in the kitchen.

"What's that? It smells great," he said, congratulating himself that he had arrived just in time for some of Mom's fried chicken.

"Sorry, that's for the dogs," my mother informed him. Don't misunderstand, she lovingly cooked mouth-watering food for her humans too, but everyone knew that her animals were considered part of the family.

My mother was worried that I wasn't feeding Susie properly. She often called me to check up on Susie and to discuss nutritional requirements and recipes. "Now, I would give her cornbread every day. Be sure to add some butter. A dog like that needs the calories. My dogs love cornbread." She tried to be tactful, but I could tell she was concerned.

Susie was a thin dog all her life, but it wasn't because she didn't eat well. I fed her special dog food for active breeds. I fed her cornbread and table scraps as my mother instructed. Susie would eat anything, but she was small for her breed and never weighed more than about forty-five pounds. Although we were surrounded by acres of woods in which she could run safely, we kept her inside the fenced dog yard part of every day so that she would have some enforced rest. As soon as she was out, off she dashed down our road at full speed, across the natural gas pipeline, along the trail by the creek, down into the valley, up the hill, and then back to the house. This long, circuitous route was her daily warm-up, just to stretch the kinks out of her legs.

How Susie loved to run, as though the very breath of life propelled her. Fortunately, she never chased cars, but she often trotted down the road accompanying Josh as he pedaled his bicycle.

"Wanna race?" Josh would ask as he pedaled harder to challenge her.

Susie always accepted the challenge and ran faster. But as he approached full speed, she seemed barely able to keep pace. She was toying with him. Josh never won a race with Susie. Just when it appeared he might pull away from her, she would stretch out her legs and leave him in her dust, flying across the land with her paws scarcely touching the earth. She might have had a great career as a hunting dog, but she probably could have done just as well at the race track.

The real business of Susie's day was to search out and chase little woodland animals. She rarely, if ever, caught anything, but the pleasure was always in the pursuit. She would dash after a squirrel, who would dart up the nearest tree and disappear into the leafy canopy from where it could safely taunt her. Susie would sit at the base of the tree, tail thumping, anticipating squirrel meat for supper. Surely, before long the squirrel would have to come down. The squirrel must have thought, *stupid dog,* as it freely scampered from treetop to treetop, being in the next county before Susie gave up and went off to hunt something else. If Susie could have been granted one wish, certainly she would have asked for the ability to climb trees.

We nicknamed her Mud Hound, because her long, wavy white fur was continually muddy and matted with burrs and leaves. Giving her a bath was a chore without rewards.

"Come here, Susie," I called to her one hot summer day. She was lying on the patio, and she eyed me suspiciously. Susie hated bath time beyond all other human inflicted rituals, and she was pretty good at reading my mind. So I was prepared.

"Look what I have for you, sweetie." I waved a piece of leftover meat. "Come and get it."

She stood up and glared at the tasty morsel. Her doubts were fully aroused, and when I took a step toward her, she knew.

No way, you can't fool me!

Off into the woods she raced.

A while later I enlisted Sam to catch her for me, and he managed to get her on a leash and brought her to where I was waiting beside the house. I put her into the dog-sized galvanized tub we kept for the purpose. Susie didn't need to talk, because her expressive brown eyes said everything.

How can you do this to me? Don't you love me? I'll never trust you again.

Her fur was nasty. I wore old clothes and was armed with plenty of shampoo, the garden hose, towels, dog brush, comb, and scissors. After shampooing and rinsing and shampooing again and more rinsing and then drying and snipping and brushing and combing and more snipping and more brushing...Susie was beautiful. Her fur hung in glorious, shiny waves with her black spots glistening upon a pristine white background. As a peace offering, I gave her the leftover meat and then released her. She took off and didn't look back. I had spent nearly two hours grooming this animal. I was sopping wet and covered with sticky fur. I stank, and I was exhausted.

About an hour later, having showered and put on fresh clothes, I looked out the kitchen window and saw her coming up from the valley. Brown muck was dripping from her belly, and a foot-long chunk of sticker bush was entangled in her tail. Gooey red clay covered her face. This stuff stains so permanently that a local company uses it to dye T-shirts they call "Alabama Dirt Shirts." Susie saw me, wagged the sticker bush, and grinned from ear to ear.

I once saw an advertisement for dog products that featured a stately English setter who wore a jeweled collar and sat regally upon a plump, silken cushion. The animal was a perfect specimen, an aristocrat who clearly lived in a world of groomers and pampered indoor comfort. What would such a dog have done with a mud hole? And could it have been half as happy as Susie?

Susie seldom came into the house. Man's abode was an alien place, and whenever she did come inside, she would shiver and shake and then bolt out the door at the first opportunity. If the weather was truly horrible, she would take shelter either inside her doghouse or the enclosed carport, but thunderstorms and freezing rain didn't bother her much. She was tough. She owned the outside world, and we humans were there to serve her and to take care of the land for her. We were to mow it and plant it and prune it so that she might enjoy it. She liked to sit on the front steps of the house, surveying her domain and watching us work.

Susie was also a sky watcher. Birds and clouds and the moon and stars forever held her fascination. I have a special birthday. It's in August, and every year on my birthday the Perseid meteor shower comes over, like fiery arrows shot from the bows of angels. Some years were better than others, but one year when the night skies were clear and promised a particularly good show, the boys and I gathered blankets and pillows and camped out on the drive in front of the house.

We snuggled between the covers and savored the heat of the asphalt, which had been gathering in the warmth of the sunshine all day, as it radiated up through our blankets. It was fun to be outside in the dark when most of our neighbors were in bed asleep. The exuberant songs of tree frogs, katydids, and crickets replaced the sounds of the day. An owl greeted us with an unearthly hoot. Mysterious grunts and groans and snaps and squeaks emanated from the woods and added to our spirit of adventure. We lay on the driveway, admiring the sparkling stars spread across the unfathomable black vault of the universe, and waited for the shiny streak of a meteor.

"There's one!"

"Where? Oh, I see it!"

"That's a good one."

As we settled down, adjusting our pillows and getting comfortable, someone cried out, "Ow, Susie, get off of me! Ooo...your nose is cold! Yikes, quit kissing me!"

There was Susie, sniffing, poking, and welcoming us with loving slurps. She nestled beside us and gazed upward, her gleaming eyes reflecting the glitter of the stars. She occasionally turned toward me, smiling, as if to say, "See, isn't this wonderful?" She seemed so happy to share her world with us. Contented, we joined together in the camaraderie of the occasion, listening to the night speech of the forest and contemplating the diamond sparkles in the dark velvety sky. Finally, in the wee hours of the morning when eyelids grew too heavy for little boys to hold open, we humans at last gathered our bedding and returned to the house, where we stumbled into our beds and then quickly fell asleep. Susie must have wondered why we did not join her more often in her nightly stargazing.

One Fourth of July, after the children had reached school age, Lou and the boys came home with a large sack of fireworks. When I was a child, my family never shot fireworks. My dad was against them. He loudly lectured us on their dangers and pronounced dire predictions of burned hands and blinded eyes, not to mention one could just as easily take a fistful of money and light it on fire. Nevertheless, I was delighted that Lou did not have the same aversion.

Assured that my husband would put safety first, I pulled a lawn chair onto the drive as Lou and the boys prepared to launch fireworks over the field between our house and the neighboring property. I was looking forward to my first personal fireworks show. But I did have one concern. How would Susie react to the shrill whistles and the booms, crackles, and pops? I had known one dog who was so frightened by the noise that it had to be sedated.

As the initial missile shrieked into the sky, Susie came to investigate, tail wagging. *What's this?* She sat down beside me, her attention focused on the dazzling display. *Wow!*

Together we watched the show as the bottle rockets, mortars, and Roman candles blasted upward and blossomed into glittering colors and intricate designs. Eyes sparkling and tongue hanging out, Susie's head went up, swiveled around, then came back down as her gaze followed the trajectory of each rocket. My own head matched her movements exactly. The ear-piercing sounds didn't bother her at all, and I wondered if this was because her ancestors had been bred to tolerate the loud discharge of gunfire.

Susie rarely participated in family barbecues or birthday parties. She might greet the guests with a friendly hello, sitting politely and offering her paw to shake, but soon she would disappear into the woods where there were more interesting things to do. However, after that first sparkly celebration, if fireworks were on the agenda, she would come running, eyes bright and tail wagging enthusiastically. She thought the colorful pyrotechnics were exclusively for her enjoyment.

Susie sometimes barked at things she saw in the trees or the sky. It could be animate or inanimate, ordinary or out of the ordinary, moving or stationary. I don't know why she did this—she did not seem disturbed or angry. Maybe she was excited about her observations and wanted to share her thoughts with the world. Her barking wasn't a huge problem, but at night we sometimes had to give her a stern word to let her know she was disturbing our peace. One evening after I had fussed and admonished her for barking, I went to check on her before turning in for the night. She lay sleeping peacefully just outside her doghouse. Then I became aware that she was making some small sounds. Was she dreaming? I listened closer and then chuckled at the soft but distinct little *arf-arf, arf-arf, arf-arf* coming from her mouth.

Susie also loved to dig. Sometimes she would be digging after a ground squirrel or other small rodent, but often she dug just for the fun of it. Susie was a master digger, not of polite little paw-sized holes, but of monster pits. We joked about training her as a backhoe. The front of her would be deep in the dirt, and the back end of her would be sticking out, hips and tail wagging wildly as the dirt came flying out of the deepening hole. One day she actually dug up several large azalea bushes. Lou was constantly filling up holes, and years after she was gone, we sometimes found old Susie holes in the woods that had to be packed with rocks and soil so that nobody would break a leg while walking across our property.

A twelve-foot-long stone planter stretches across the front of our house beneath the living room windows, and I envisioned it filled with colorful flowers that overflowed and draped down in front of the stones. I had once seen a photo of a French chateau with a stone planter spilling over with exuberant blooms, inspiring me to try for a similar look, though I admitted that my own peculiar wooden house, with its long central eyebrow that overhung the planter, did not quite match the charm of a French chateau!

When we lived in the tree house, we had a somewhat smaller planter beside the slanting walk leading up to the front door. I once tried to plant flowers in it, but I had no success. This was because of Josh. Before children, I had grown flowers in numerous pots on our wraparound deck and inside the screened porch. But potted plants are high-maintenance, and after Sam and then Josh came along, I realized I had to grow either children or plants. I couldn't do both. But with one child at last out of diapers, I decided a few flowers in the big planter would be manageable.

That year, when he was about two, Josh looked on as I planted a flat of pink petunias in the planter. I lifted each baby petunia out of its little black plastic container and placed it in the hole I had carefully prepared, then scooped soil around it. I watered them in when I finished, and Josh and I admired them. Some were beginning to bloom already, so there was lots of promise. I turned to other yard work, and Josh puttered along beside me. I must not have been watching him as closely as I thought, because when I glanced back at the planter a while later, something didn't seem quite right. I looked closer and was flabbergasted to find every petunia lying out of its hole, wilted under the hot noonday sun.

Josh held up one of the flowers and smiled. Josh has a smile to soften the stony heart of a statue. It is his best feature. "I picked them for you," he said.

The planter remained empty.

But now Josh was four years old and knew better than to pull up Mom's flowers, so I could safely try again. I confidently filled the stone planter with a multicolored array of petunias, marigolds, and other easy-to-grow flowers. I stepped back and imagined the romantic effect they would have when fully mature—what a nice welcome they would present to visitors coming to the front door.

The next day I found my flowers cast aside in a pile, and Susie glared at me defiantly from a newly dug out doggie bed inside the planter. I looked into her eyes, and I knew I had a problem.

"NO! NO! Bad dog!" I scolded her with the sternest voice possible, and Susie slunk away with her tail between her legs. I salvaged as many flowers as possible and replanted them.

I opened the front door the next morning and gasped. All of my flowers had completely disappeared, and Susie was lying in another hole. A snarl came from between my gritted teeth. I lunged for her with intent to commit canine murder, but Susie was much too swift. She escaped into the woods as I shouted out descriptions of her gruesome demise if I ever, ever caught her in my planter again.

And so began the War of the Planter. Later that day I was driving home from an errand, and as I rounded the curve and the house came into view, I spotted Susie relaxing in the planter, her head peeking out over the edge of her hole as she surveyed the terrain. Our eyes locked, and she gave me the wild, startled look of a sinner caught in the act. Before I could slow the car, she jumped out of the planter and raced into the woods.

Daily battles continued for months. It wasn't that Susie couldn't learn. She was intelligent, and she knew I had banned her from digging in the planter. But she disagreed with me. She was a stubborn dog, and in her mind the planter was part of her territory. From there she had a great view of the property, and clearly it was also the perfect place to settle in for a nap.

She began to avoid me. Whenever I walked outside, she would slink past me, eyeing me with complaint and accusation as she headed toward the forest. Nevertheless, as soon as the coast was clear, she would hurry back and start digging in her favorite forbidden spot. Many times as I walked through the living room I would glance out the window, and there she would be, curled up comfortably in a nice doggie hole. Every time I opened the front door to scold her, she would sprint away.

Lou and I came up with the idea of sprinkling the planter with some prickly sweet gum balls. I thought the spiky fruit would surely deter Susie. I was so tired of those ugly pits and torn plants right beside the front door, and it would be good to finally have flowers. (Looking back, I can't believe we did this. Sweet gum balls can get stuck in a dog's paw and cause injury. It was a stupid thing to do. Despite my threats, I did not want any harm to come to Susie.)

So we scattered the sweet gum balls throughout the planter. The next morning I walked into the living room and looked outside. I stood with my arms crossed over my chest and shook my head.

"I don't believe it."

Susie was in the planter, lying in a newly dug doggie hole, snuggled up like a baby in a bassinet. Susie was smarter than we were, and she saved us from our stupidity. We found every one of the sweet gum balls piled together in a neat heap to the side.

I acknowledged defeat and gave up on growing flowers in the planter. I eventually put in some spreading junipers that coexisted peacefully with Susie. Landscape contractors use these tough evergreen shrubs in difficult situations to prevent soil erosion. Even Susie could not kill a spreading juniper. She would dig between them and lie peacefully amidst the greenery. The shrubs flourished and the low-growing, horizontal branches hid the holes that Susie dug. We declared a truce, and the War of the Planter came to an end.

Years later, after Susie was gone, I wrote the following children's poem as a memorial to her:

Susie's World

Down into the dirt
Where little worms dwell,
Where plants spread their roots, and the earth has a smell
That is rich and good,
Susie is digging:
Digging for bony treasure or buried toy
And just for the pleasure.
Oh! The joy!

Her head and shoulders are thrust into the hole
That her paws are making.
Her rear end is shaking, shaking
And her tail is wagging, wagging
As the dirt comes flying, flying
Up out of the deepening hole.
Susie is a happy dog.

Josh jumps on his bike and goes for a ride.
Susie comes running, running.
Her legs propel her. She catches up to Josh and runs by his side.
They pass a field of wildflowers and some towering trees,
A giant ant hill and busy, buzzing bees.
A hawk soars above in the great blue sky.
Josh pedals his bike faster, faster, and Susie flies.
All is right in the world for Susie and her boy.
As she is running, running,
Susie is a happy dog.

Susie is barking, barking.
It is 2AM.
She barks at the moon.
She barks at a light.
She barks at strange noises from things out of sight.
She barks at an owl perched in a tree,
And she barks at gold eyes peeking through the leaves.
She is barking, barking
Until,
Finally,
A voice from inside sounds out, "Be quiet!

No more barking for you, Susie!
Go to your doghouse for the rest of the night!"
So Susie goes to sleep,
And in her dreams she is barking, barking.
Susie is a happy dog.

Susie is getting a bath.
She sits in a washtub with soap on her face.
She is NOT a happy dog. Dirty water surrounds her.
She wants to be some other place!
The water is rising, rising.
It's over her knees!
Hands keep scrubbing, scrubbing and pulling at her fur.
Hands hose her down. She shivers and shakes.
It's awful what sacrifices a dog has to make
To live with her humans.
Susie, at last, is clean and patted dry.
Her fur is brushed to a shine, and Susie looks FINE.
Now she is free!
Into the woods!
Into the mud hole!
Susie is a happy dog.

There are wonderful things in Susie's world:
Birds above and lots of squirrels.
Things to chase and things to smell.
Food for the belly,
And a forest full of trails.
A family that loves her.
Susie sits with her boy on the front steps.

Susie

She rests her head against his knee.
They are watching the world.
The sun is setting.
Susie is a happy, happy dog.

CHAPTER THREE

SHEPHERD

"Hey, Mom! Come see!"

We had been settled into our new home in Helena a few months and Susie was a growing puppy, when one day Sam and Josh called to me from outside. I looked out the kitchen door, and my heart skipped a beat.

My little children had their arms wrapped around the body of a great beast. I opened the door and stepped out. The animal was grinning and thumping its thick tail good-naturedly, but its jaws easily could have encircled a small boy's head.

"Look, Mom! He's real friendly. What kind is he?" The boys smiled as they hugged the visitor.

"He's a German shepherd," I replied as I tried to stay calm. *And probably part grizzly bear too.* He was the biggest dog I had ever seen up close and personal. "You shouldn't touch a strange dog. He might not like it. He could bite you."

"He won't bite. He's nice. See!" They stroked the animal, running their hands through his thick black and tan fur, and in response he plopped down and rolled over onto his back, patting the air with his front paws and wanting some more cuddling.

"Can we keep him?"

"Of course not. We already have a dog, and I'm sure he already has a home." I reached down and petted him, and the great beast gazed into my eyes. He had a noble face. He was magnificent.

"Look. He has a collar with tags," I pointed out to the boys. "That means he has a family that loves him. He probably lives in one of those houses on the other side of the woods."

The next day the dog returned, and the next day after that, and the next and the next. He spent hours playing with Sam and Josh. Susie, too, romped with him, and he followed her through the woods as she introduced him to interesting features of her territory. I watched while the two dogs poked their heads under shrubs and dug around rocks together, then lay companionably beside one another when they became tired. I was uneasy about the situation and finally called the phone number on the tag.

"Your German shepherd is spending a lot of time at our house," I explained. "He's not causing any problems, but I thought you would like to know where he is."

"Shepherd? Oh, he's a great dog, isn't he?" the man on the other end of the phone exclaimed. "But he's not exactly my dog. He showed up in our neighborhood last year. We tried to find the owner, but nobody claimed him. Several of us feed him, and I took him and got his shots, but he travels around visiting all of us. He stays wherever he wants. Everybody loves him. You could say that he belongs to the whole neighborhood."

So Shepherd didn't have a home after all. Not really. I was concerned about him. The vagabond lifestyle he had established for himself was hazardous. Automobiles moved up and down the streets of the suburban neighborhood where he roamed. Upon close inspection Shepherd did not seem completely healthy. His coat was dull. He had fleas. Lou and I looked at each other.

"He's a wonderful dog," Lou said.

"Yes, he is."

One day Shepherd showed up with a pellet gun wound in his hip. So not everybody loved him. Someone did not want this large dog wandering about the property. Or maybe there was an angry teenager, aiming at a big target. After a quick family conference, I called the phone number on the tag again.

"Look, somebody up there is shooting at Shepherd. Let us have him. We have over three acres for him to play in. We live at the dead end of a private road. There are woods all around, and there's no traffic. He gets along well with our other dog, and our children love him. We'll take good care of him, and he'll be safe."

"I'll have to talk to some of my neighbors. I'll call you back," the man said.

The neighborhood friends of Shepherd talked among themselves and agreed that Shepherd needed a permanent, secure home.

The next day our phone rang. "He's yours," the man said, and we all cheered.

We took Shepherd to our vet for a checkup and learned that he was about two years old. He was a gentle giant. Solid, big-boned and muscular, he weighed in at one hundred and ten pounds, much more than the combined weights of both my children. But he obediently lay on the examining table and allowed the vet to poke and prod and perform outrageous indignities. He did hate the shots. Nevertheless, when the needle went in, all he did was lift his head and let out a long, pitiful "Ahh-roo-ooo".

Shepherd now wore new tags with our phone number on them. He was officially our dog. I decided to keep Shepherd inside the dog yard a portion of each day, just as we did with Susie. I thought we could let him out when we were home to watch over him. I opened the gate and led him into the lot, but when I went out and closed the gate behind me, Shepherd began to bark and howl. Then he hurled his body against the fence again and again. Shaken and worried that he would injure himself, I opened the gate and let him out. Shepherd happily spent most of his time with us, and he always came home at night. But we were concerned because he still liked to call on his old buddies up in the neighborhood. His friends welcomed him warmly, and apparently none of them discouraged him. Ultimately, that would lead to a lot of grief.

We were expecting our third child. I watched Shepherd play with Sam and Josh. What would he think about a baby? We were delighted with our growing family, and we started making changes to accommodate the new arrival. The old two-door Chevy Nova, my first major purchase after graduating from college, already had two booster seats strapped into the back. The vehicle had a 175-horsepower 350-cubic-inch V-8 engine, and it was destined to leave behind its staid position as a family car to become a young man's hot rod. I had paid thirty-two hundred dollars for it, new, in 1973. Now, twelve years later, we sold it for fifteen hundred and bought our first minivan, a

Ford Aerostar. Minivans were a popular new breed of car, recently introduced to the world to fit the needs of growing families like ours.

Almost everyone thought the baby would be a girl. Before I had children, my friends assured me I was the kind of person who would have girls. I don't know what criteria they were using. After we moved to Helena, we had one extra bedroom, and it had beautiful pink wallpaper. Surely, the argument went, this was a sign from God.

I wasn't so sure; I had a feeling that this child would be another boy. I had an ultrasound when I was six months pregnant, and I was eager to find out what the baby's sex was so that I could get rid of the pink wallpaper before the baby's birth if it was a boy. But the child's legs were drawn up and firmly crossed, and the technician wouldn't even make a guess. Ultrasounds weren't so common in those days, so that was my only shot to find out.

Josh, age four, was the one person who openly wanted a boy. "That way we'll have three brothers," he said.

I had a dream in which I saw a newborn baby boy who looked up and smiled. While everyone around me praised the wonders of little girls, secretly I agreed with Josh.

One cold day in January, the time came. As we were heading to the hospital, I said to Lou, "You know, this could be another boy. Don't you think we should pick out a boy name, just in case?"

We had previously mentioned various boy names, but most of the talk had been about girls. Girl names were easy. There were at least a half-dozen girl names that I liked. Boy names were difficult. With both of my first two children I was well into my ninth month before we settled on a boy name. Now, with the third one, I was in labor, and we had not made a final decision.

"How about Mark Edward?" Lou asked.

"Sounds good to me." I probably would have agreed to any name at that moment, as another labor contraction began.

Just as I expected, Mark Edward arrived early the next morning. It was January 8th—Elvis Presley's birthday. (Every year when Mark's birthday came around, my mother, a huge Elvis fan, would remind me of the significance of the date, lest I forget this important fact.) Lou was holding Mark only moments after the birth when the infant looked straight up into his dad's eyes and gave a huge smile. Scientists say these early smiles are "gas smiles." Nope. It was a genuine smile. He was the baby of my dream. We brought Mark home and put him in the pink bedroom, where he lived contentedly for ten months, until at last we got around to changing the decor to navy blue and white.

Spring comes early to our part of the world, and Mark was only a few weeks old when I put him in the stroller and pushed him down the road for his first outing. He was swaddled in blankets and a cap was pulled low over his forehead. Comfortably warm and lulled by the movement of the stroller, Mark was soon drowsing. Clumps of yellow daffodils were blooming, and tiny, chartreuse green buds were swelling along the branches of shrubs and trees. The crystal blue sky carried wisps of fluffy clouds. I filled my lungs with the cool, crisp air. It was great to be out again.

As I was pushing the stroller, I saw Shepherd bounding toward me. I had not yet introduced Mark to him. I waited nervously for his reaction when he halted in front of us. He put his great head into the stroller and sniffed at the strange human creature in front of him.

I petted him. "This is Mark," I told him.

Mark opened his eyes and squinted at the furry face a few inches from his own. Shepherd gave a final sniff, then sat and thumped his tail. I resumed my walk, and Shepherd stayed protectively beside me.

He thereby appointed himself as our guardian, and from that day onward he accompanied Mark and me on our daily strolls.

Any dog can be dangerous. Shepherd took his role of protector seriously, and I am sure he would have attacked anybody who threatened a member of my family. One day Shepherd quietly approached as I talked to a man whom I had hired to do some work on the house. The carpenter was a good person with a family and pets of his own, and Shepherd was OK with me talking to him. He didn't bark or show any aggression toward the man. Nevertheless, just in case, he positioned himself so that he was between the man and myself, politely conveying the message that the guy would have to go through him to get to me. While we strolled around the house discussing needed repairs, Shepherd walked with us, constantly keeping his body between the two of us.

Shepherd was accustomed to mail carriers and delivery people. These persons came and went routinely under Shepherd's friendly but watchful eye. He never chased or jumped on people and rarely barked except to say hello. Some people were afraid of Shepherd. He usually greeted strangers with a wagging tail and maybe a welcoming bark. But even his friendliest bark was deep and loud, and his size usually intimidated people who didn't know him. I once walked out of the house to discover a UPS guy crouched upon the hood of his big truck. Shepherd was below him, bouncing around, barking but with welcoming overtones. I could tell that my dog was in his "How you doing, let's play!" mode, but the man thought his life was in jeopardy.

I understand it, but size discrimination seems unfair. Most of the large dogs I have known have been sweethearts, while some tiny dogs would have been happy to eat me alive if given the opportunity. I once stood behind a woman in the grocery checkout line. She carried a miniature dachshund in a handbag. The little dog was wearing a fuzzy, baby blue sweater. The tiny face peeked at me over the edge of the bag.

"Oh, how cute!" I cooed. The animal curled its lip and gave me the evil eye.

"Grrrrrrrrrrrrr." *I am not cute!*

I held Shepherd by the collar and coaxed the UPS guy down from his truck. "He has a loud bark, but he's just saying hello. He won't hurt you."

The delivery man slipped to the ground and chuckled a bit, but he maintained his distance as he hastily dropped our package on the carport, then leaped back into his truck.

Shepherd was one of the best security systems we could have had. While Susie was inherently trustful of humans, Shepherd had the look and the instincts of a guard dog. One day a young man—rather scruffy with faded, torn jeans, long hair, and a beard—drove up in a pickup truck. Maybe he was a nice person, or maybe he wasn't. He got out of the truck, walked around the house and proceeded toward the kitchen door. About that time, I heard Shepherd barking ferociously and decided I had better see what was happening. I looked out the kitchen's glass door.

The man was frozen. Shepherd was crouched about ten feet in front of him, his body and tail rigid, a menacing growl coming from his throat. I opened the door.

"I just came to read the meter," the man whispered.

Shepherd looked up at me, questioning, and the man took the opportunity to pull out a can of mace and spray it in his direction. Shepherd backed away a few feet, and the guy quickly departed. He may have been a legitimate meter reader. The electricity meter is located near the kitchen door, so he probably was telling the truth.

But I don't know for sure. I never saw him again, and Shepherd never again reacted that way toward any utility or service person.

Shepherd adored women. For a woman, Shepherd would sit and offer his paw to shake. He would roll over. He would plop his great head in her lap—anything to gain her affection. We speculated that his original owner must have been a woman. One dreary, cool day a woman came to the front door taking some kind of survey. She wore a dark business suit and carried a briefcase. It was a bad time for me. Sam was lying on the living room couch, sick with strep throat. Mark was needing some attention and a diaper change, and Josh was waiting for his lunch. Chilly mist was in the air. I should have told the woman that I couldn't help her, but she insisted that the survey was important (I don't remember what it was about).

"I'll only take a few minutes of your time. Can I come inside?" she asked.

"No, I'm sorry. I have a sick child," I replied. "We can stand out here." I moved out onto the porch and shut the door behind me.

Shepherd came around the corner of the house and saw us. He stopped on the walkway and began to bark, but not his usual welcoming bark. There was deep warning in his tone.

"I think we should go into the house," the woman said nervously as Shepherd's bark became louder and more insistent.

"No, this really isn't a good time." What was it was about this person that Shepherd didn't like?

"I won't take long. Please let's go inside just a minute."

Shepherd continued to bark fiercely and moved a few steps closer to us. While I could sympathize with her anxiety, I was not going to let that woman inside my house.

"I'm sorry. You should go. I can't help you today."

The woman mumbled something and then turned toward her car. Shepherd followed her, barking incessantly, and then stood on the drive and barked at the car as she drove away. How strange. Shepherd had never barked like that at a woman before (and very few men, for that matter). Maybe he sensed that in some way she was a threat to me, or maybe he was just telling her that today we were too stressed out to answer a survey.

Susie got along well with other dogs that sometimes wandered across our property. She must have had a good doggie personality. She had accepted Shepherd from the beginning, and the two quickly became best friends. She tried to teach him to hunt, and he diligently tried to learn. One morning I saw Susie by the edge of the woods. She was pointing like any good hunting dog, her tail stiff and front paw raised. Shepherd was beside her, tail stiff and front paw raised in perfect imitation. But when Susie darted into the forest, her apprentice awkwardly lumbered after her, crashing through shrubs and struggling over boulders and other obstacles that she leaped over easily. He had no hope of keeping up and soon was standing alone, wondering to where in the world Susie and whatever it was she was chasing had disappeared.

It was Sam who became Shepherd's hunting partner. Together they explored the woods and valley, seeking curious living things to examine or to catch. They discovered multicolored salamanders hiding under rocks, they caught snakes slithering through tall weeds, and they relentlessly pursued ground squirrels into underground burrows. They captured possums, mice, and turtles and then released them, or sometimes they brought the critters home for admiration or care.

One afternoon I looked out the kitchen window and saw the top of Sam's head as he was coming up out of the valley. First, his bobbing curls appeared over the ridge, then his face and neck, shoulders and arms, and finally the rest of him. His arms were spread wide. In one hand he clutched a long black snake, holding it firmly behind the neck as it dangled nearly to the ground. In the other hand he triumphantly held a box turtle. Shepherd was beside him, and Sam's face bore the wide grin of a successful hunter.

An abandoned farmhouse from another era, weather-beaten and grown over with kudzu, stood near the end of our road where it intersects with the highway. Several acres of pasture surrounded the old house, and a small number of horses boarded on the property. To my consternation, Shepherd became interested in these big animals. At every opportunity he would slip under the barbed wire fence. Back and forth he would dart, circling the horses, barking and barely escaping their hooves.

"I wish he would quit harassing those horses," I said to Lou one afternoon when we walked down the road and saw him dancing around the animals.

"No, watch him. There's a real method to his movement. I think he's trying to round them up."

"Huh, I think you're right. His ancestors were bred to herd farm animals, so I guess it's instinctive." Maybe Shepherd thought a horse would be a fine prize to bring home.

Sam had compassion for all of God's little creatures, and often he brought orphaned or injured animals to me for assistance. A lot of times they were orphaned or injured because of Shepherd. Shepherd attacked, then Sam rescued. They were a great team. The two of them would come home together, Shepherd not looking at all guilty, Sam simply full of concern for the needy animal in his hands.

We became regular visitors to the wildlife rescue center located at Oak Mountain State Park not far from our home, where dedicated volunteers worked twenty four hours a day to doctor and feed injured and orphaned wildlife. Under such nurturing attention, most of the baby birds, possums, and other wild animals that Sam and Shepherd "rescued" survived and later were able to return to the wild.

Sometimes we cared for the creatures ourselves. I was talking on the phone one day when Sam tapped me on the shoulder. I turned around to see him holding a three foot long snake in his hands. By then I was well into my training in the art of raising boys, so I didn't scream or throw the phone across the room.

"What a pretty snake," I said.

The creature was black with gold stripes down its side. I knew that it was a harmless eastern garter snake. Snakes have an important place in a balanced ecosystem, and my philosophy about them is to let them live their lives unless they are a threat. I ended my phone conversation and turned back to my son.

"You need to let him go, Sam. He's a great snake, but he needs to be free."

"But he's hurt!" Sam, always so full of devilment, looked at me with pleading eyes.

I considered my son. He was dressed in faded jeans and a red T-shirt. His beautiful curly hair was like a halo encircling his angelic face. (Sam kept those curls for years, though he wore his hair shorter while he was in high school. As a college freshman he let it grow longer again, and I smiled to see those familiar ringlets bouncing when he moved. Then one day he came home with a shaved head. Surprised, I asked why he had done this to his hair, and he replied that the girls would not quit playing with it.)

I looked closer at the snake. Sure enough, there was a long, oozing wound on its side. I sighed. "Well, let's put him in a box for now, and we'll see what Dad says when he comes home."

Sometimes passing the buck is a good thing to do. We lined a large cardboard box with old towels and put the snake in it. We put the box in the home office at the back of the house. What a nice surprise Lou would have.

When Lou drove up later that day, Sam ran out to greet him. I didn't hear anything for about ten minutes. Then Lou came into the kitchen.

"I need some Neosporin and some bandages," he said.

My mouth must have hung open, because he paused a moment, then added, "You realize I'm doing this for Sam, not the snake."

In that moment I remembered why I loved my husband so much.

Lou doctored the snake and allowed Sam to keep it in his office. The next morning, I smelled a putrid odor emanating from that part of the house—the wounded snake was stinking to high heaven. Fortunately, in a couple of days the cut was healing nicely, and Sam took the snake back down into the valley and released it. We opened the windows to let Lou's office air out and sprayed some air freshener in it, and soon it was back to normal too.

Not all snakes were so lucky. The time Sam and Shepherd brought home an angry copperhead, the back of its neck clutched tightly in one of Sam's bare hands and its tail in the other, we weren't so compassionate. Alabama has a few indigenous venomous snakes, and the copperhead is one of them. Sam knew it was dangerous, which is why he was holding it so carefully, but he didn't fully understand the risk.

"Please help this snake," he begged. It, too, had been injured.

Lou helped it all right—he got a shovel and helped it move on to its eternal reward. After that, Sam never brought home another poisonous snake.

As a mother, I always wanted to protect my children and to keep them safe. I was glad that Shepherd accompanied Sam on his expeditions into the wild parts of our neighborhood. I knew this gallant dog would defend my son, no matter what, and if anything ever happened to him, Shepherd would let me know. Life is unpredictable, however, and there were some things from which neither Shepherd nor I could protect Sam.

CHAPTER FOUR

ᗪᴀʀᴋ Sʜᴀᴅᴏᴡꜱ

Two years after Mark's birth, I was expecting another baby. We had felt that our family was complete with three boys, so this was a big surprise. What an adjustment. Lou didn't speak to me for four days, although he certainly had as much to do with it as I did. But soon we both accepted that our family was growing again, and we began to look forward to the new addition. I was seventeen weeks pregnant when I had an ultrasound, and the technician smiled and said, "She looks great, very healthy."

"She?"

Were we going to have a little girl, after all? I added it up: a husband, three boys, a girl (finally!), two dogs, a tankful of fish, plus whatever odd assortment of wild critters any given day would present—life was going to be full, indeed. We began making plans. I was wishing I had the pretty pink bedroom back. Where would we put a girl child, and how would that girl fit in with all the male creatures? I went out and bought new maternity clothes. It was good to feel the stir of new life again, cradled protectively inside my womb.

A week later Sam became ill with flu-like symptoms. So did I. We weren't terribly ill, just the typical headache, fever, and muscle aches. Until one night I was in bed covered up with blankets and shaking with chills, and for just a moment I felt a wild fluttering down low in my abdomen.

This is going to kill the baby.

The words popped into my consciousness, heartless and unbidden, from some dark recess of my mind. I immediately pushed the shocking thought away. I had never heard of flu being fatal to the unborn.

However, I did not feel the baby move again after that night. (I later read some research that concluded that influenza, especially with high fever, can cause problems for a fetus.) When I went to the doctor, the terrible truth was confirmed. The baby was dead. This was on a Monday. Sam and Josh were out of school for spring break.

Sam developed an earache and was diagnosed with an ear infection on Tuesday. He was put on antibiotics for that, but otherwise he seemed to have recovered from his own illness. Everybody was caught up in the tragedy of the baby, and no one was paying particular attention to him.

Lou accompanied me to the hospital on Wednesday, and my parents stayed with the boys until he returned home that evening. I was discharged from the hospital the next day. My baby girl was gone.

The loving faces of my family would be the best therapy I could have, and Lou brought the boys with him when he came to pick me up.

"Sam's been nauseated. He threw up his supper last night," Lou mentioned as we drove down the highway.

"I feel fine now. I'm hungry!" Sam responded.

"What do you feel like eating?" I asked.

"A hamburger with fries," he said, so we stopped at McDonald's on the way home and got that for him.

He ate it greedily, but soon after we returned home he vomited again. Was this some stomach bug? Additional symptoms of the flu? Nevertheless, except for throwing up, he didn't seem too ill. This was on Thursday. I remember what happened every day that week.

Friday morning I went outside and briefly visited with Susie and Shepherd. I hugged them and rubbed my hands over their warm bodies, pulling them close and gaining some comfort from their sniffs and nuzzles. Could they read my facial expression? Did they have an inherent ability to sense the loss I felt? They huddled close and seemed to understand my mood. But after a while I returned to the house. Exhausted, I climbed back under the covers and stayed in bed the rest of the day with my dark and sad thoughts.

Sam spent most of Friday outside playing. That evening he asked if he could use my bathroom to take a shower because the boys' bath was already in use. When he came out dressed only in his underwear, I stared at him, stunned. I hadn't looked closely at him all week, and now it seemed that overnight he had turned into a skeleton. I hurried him onto the bathroom scale. Sam weighed forty-two pounds. When I had last checked it, his weight had been fifty-four pounds.

Something was wrong, and I experienced a profound sense of foreboding. I could feel our family being pulled into a dismal place of darkening shadows, a place of trials and weary sorrow, a place where carefree happy life was only painful memory. A place where the Grim Reaper lives.

On Saturday morning I took Sam to the doctor. This was flu season, and sick children and their parents crowded into the rectangular waiting room. We were fortunate to find small plastic chairs while we waited. Some people were standing up, and some were sitting on the floor. There was only one pediatrician in the office that day, and we waited a long time. My concern was growing. Sam was feeling worse, and he complained of blurred vision. He had vomited again.

We finally saw the physician. Dr. Jenkins (not his real name) was covering for our regular pediatrician that weekend. He wiped beads of sweat from his brow as he hurried into the room. He had never seen my son before, and he didn't believe me when I told him that Sam had lost twelve pounds.

"Oh, now Sam is a thin kid anyway," he said as he looked at the weight recorded on Sam's chart from the previous year. He ordered blood and urine tests, and we sat alone in the examining room as we waited for the results.

After about thirty minutes, Dr. Jenkins returned. "Well, he's not as sick as we feared," he said brightly. "He has gastroenteritis, and this on top of the flu and ear infection has been tough on his system. You need to put him to bed. He's a bit dehydrated. Give him lots of fluids. Gatorade, juices, cola, whatever he'll take. I think he'll be just fine. Call me if he gets worse." Dr. Jenkins had a calm and reassuring manner. He gave us medicine for nausea and sent us home.

Why don't I feel good about this? Despite the doctor's words, I was troubled. I looked at Sam slumped in the passenger's side of the car as I drove home. My gut told me that we had missed something.

Sam did not improve. The more juices we gave him, the more he vomited. He complained of abdominal pain. I called the doctor's office and spoke with Dr. Jenkins again. He reassured me that all was well and to keep doing what we were doing. But as the afternoon progressed, Sam sometimes seemed delirious, and I was increasingly fearful that something dreadful was happening. I called the doctor back.

My exact words to Dr. Jenkins were, "I am extremely concerned about his metabolic status. I have never seen my child, or any child, this sick outside of a hospital." I should have reminded him that I was a nurse. Maybe he would have listened to me.

"Now, I saw Sam this morning," the doctor said, obviously thinking I was being a bit hysterical, "and I don't believe he's that sick. If he seems disoriented, it's because of the nausea medicine. Sometimes it does that. Don't give him any more, and let's see if he doesn't improve."

Lou was worried about me as well as his son. I was still experiencing physical problems associated with of the loss of the baby, and I was emotionally distraught. I had scarcely slept in a week. He convinced me to go to bed, and he promised to watch over Sam. I somehow was able to fall into a fitful sleep. Several hours later, I woke up suddenly. I could hear Sam's breathing, all the way from the other side of the house. It was about midnight. Lou came into the room and smiled.

"Sam's better," he said. "He's not throwing up any more. He drank some milkshake, and he's sleeping now."

I walked into Sam's room. His breathing was very slow, deep and labored. I had heard that breathing before in certain hospitalized patients.

"Oh, dear God, he's in a coma."

Lou just looked at me. He had no words.

I shook Sam's shoulders and tried to waken him.

"Sam! Sam!" I was frantic.

At last he opened his eyelids and glanced up at me. His dark eyes were sunken deep into his face and were surrounded by bluish-black circles.

"I'm scared," he whispered, then shut his eyes again and lapsed back into unconsciousness.

I called the doctor's answering service. "Dr. Jenkins may think I'm crazy, but you tell him," I said to the woman who took his messages, "that my son is in a coma, and I believe he is going to die."

Lou wrapped Sam in the green and red quilt from his bed and then carried him out to the car. He drove to the emergency room of Children's Hospital in Birmingham while I waited anxiously at home, crying and praying. Josh and Mark continued to sleep soundly.

Lou called me from the hospital two hours later. They had been the longest hours of my life.

"Sam's going to be fine," he said. "He has diabetes. He's in a coma—but he's in the intensive care unit, and he's receiving treatment. He's going to be OK."

Diabetes? I was dazed, but also somewhat relieved. A person can live with diabetes. I had feared some awful acute form of cancer or other fatal illness. But diabetes? The pediatrician had checked Sam's blood and urine, and he easily should have diagnosed diabetes in the office.

Lou assured me that he would be home to look after Josh and Mark so that I could be at the hospital for the next visiting hour. I was dressed and ready long before he arrived.

Later that day, I felt numb while I sat in the ICU with Sam and watched him breathe. He was still unconscious. The green and red quilt from home covered the hospital bed sheets. He was in a quiet part of the ICU, and the nurses let me stay with him, although visitors were usually limited to certain times. Assorted wires, IV lines, and catheters ran from his body, and he was surrounded by pumps and monitors. Odd, me being a nurse, but I wasn't interested in those technical things. I knew mothers who kept detailed notes of daily treatments and tests when their children were hospitalized. I wanted only to look at my son, taking in his beautiful face and thanking God for his life.

It had been close. Initially, the emergency room doctor who took care of Sam had treated Lou badly.

"Why in the world did you wait so long to bring this child in?"

Why, indeed? Questions swirled in my mind. The strong fruity smell—much like acetone—that characterizes uncontrolled diabetes was overwhelming, permeating the air around Sam's bed. Why hadn't we noticed that odor at home? Probably because he was throwing up all that fruit juice we were pouring down him, and we attributed the smell to that.

What about other symptoms of diabetes, like thirst and frequent urination? Who was paying attention to how much a child drank or peed that week?

Why hadn't I insisted that Lou take Sam to the hospital much earlier in the day when his symptoms had worsened? Why had I not paid attention to my instincts?

I looked up from Sam's bedside and saw Dr. Jenkins.

"I have some things to say to you," I told him.

He nodded. Every doctor makes mistakes. He wasn't a bad doctor, but I hope he became a better doctor after what happened with Sam. He had been so rushed, so busy the day before that he had not really looked at my son or listened to what I said.

Dr. Jenkins did not try to make excuses. He explained that he had misread the lab results when he glanced at the report, which had been hastily scribbled by the lab technician.

"I told you that I was worried about Sam's metabolic status and that I had never seen a child this sick outside of a hospital."

The doctor shook his head. "I heard those words." He shut his eyes and repeated, "I heard those words."

But Dr. Jenkins did say something that I appreciated and held close to my heart for many years to come. "Our goal now is to keep Sam healthy and to make this the last hospitalization he ever has for diabetes."

Sam was in a coma most of that day. When he woke up, we entered a routine of multiple daily insulin injections, finger pricks throughout both day and night to monitor blood sugar, and careful management of diet and exercise. Type 1 diabetes (also called insulin-dependent and juvenile diabetes) is a twenty-four hour, around-the-clock illness, and one can never take a vacation from it. High blood sugars can damage blood vessels and vital organs and can lead to coma and death. Low blood sugars affect the brain and can cause behavior changes, seizure, unconsciousness, brain damage...and death. The aim is to keep the blood sugar levels as close to normal as possible. I was overcome by the magnitude of what we would have to do, every day, from now on, forever.

Sam took it all in stride, and he had fun during his hospital stay. After he was well enough to leave the ICU, he was transferred to the adolescent unit. At age seven, he was the youngest patient on the floor. He became the nurses' pet, and they lavished him with attention.

"Miss Nancy," my friend from church, had given Sam a pair of flip-flops shaped like dinosaur feet. They were too big for him, but he insisted on wearing them. He explored the halls, and you could hear him coming—flap, flap, flap. He felt like hot stuff, making friends with all the teenagers and learning to play video games.

We had a new pediatrician whose special interest was diabetes. Dr. Jamie was good medicine for us. She was in her thirties, a petite woman with a large, upbeat personality. She exuded energy and positivity. I thought of a camp counselor when she bounced into Sam's hospital room with a smile and enthusiastic greeting. It was easy to envision her leading a pack of kids along a mountain trail or taking a group of teenagers on a whitewater rafting trip.

Dr. Jamie made us feel special. I have since found out that she made most of her patients feel that way. It was her gift.

Only a few days after we met her, she began teaching Sam how to give a shot. After watching Sam give several stabs at an orange, she rolled up her sleeve and let him practice on her own arm. I held my breath as Sam confidently jabbed the needle into his new doctor's upper arm. Without a flinch, she praised his great shot-giving ability. Sam beamed.

"Would you like to give one to yourself?" Dr. Jamie then asked my seven-year-old son.

No problem. He was hot stuff.

After a week of hospitalization, Sam was ready for discharge. Before we left, he walked—flap, flap, flap—to the intensive care unit to say good-by to the doctors and nurses there. He stared wide-eyed at the place from which he had come. A few machines alternately beeped, wheezed, and clicked in the background. He couldn't really see the children who were lying in the beds. They were hidden behind rails and covered with sheets and various medical paraphernalia. He hugged the staff, and they all fussed over him and said how happy they were to see him doing well. Then he turned and—flap, flap, flap—headed back down the hall. It was time to go home.

So we went home, and life returned to normal. Normal? How could life be normal? *I hate this*, I thought, as I poked my son with needles. I rebelled at the thought of doing this, over and over and over again. I rebelled at the thought of counting carbohydrates and watching every bite of food my son ate. I'm a nurse, and that fact did not make things easier.

But surrounded by the accouterments and demands of daily life, we did settle into a new normal, eventually. God's light overcomes the darkness, and lifted up by love and many prayers, we received strength to climb out of that dark place and back into the light. But I was aware of the shadows as I had never been before, and I knew that in this world they would always be lurking. But life went on. We did what we had to do, because we had to.

A couple days after returning home, I saw Sam heading into the forest with Shepherd. I opened my mouth to call out, to tell him he couldn't go exploring by himself anymore. What if something happened to him while he was out there? What if his blood sugar dropped too low and he passed out? Yet I hesitated. I couldn't keep him beside me the rest of his life. But he was only seven years old.

Parenthood is filled with difficult choices. It was a tough decision, but I closed my mouth and allowed him to go explore the woods with his dog. I decided that we would do everything in our power to control this disease, but I determined that it would not control us. Sam would live a full and normal life. So I watched my child disappear into the woods, reassured that at least he had Shepherd with him.

One day a storm came up while Sam and Shepherd were in the forest together. I hurried outside.

"Sam! Sam! Come inside! Now!"

Susie returned from one of her own forays into the woods and headed toward the carport as black clouds boiled over the earth, but Sam and Shepherd did not appear. I called out again. The shrill wind blew my words away, and I shouted louder. There was no response. The thick atmosphere had a greenish-gray cast, and thunderclaps beat the air. I was worried. This was a bad storm. Lightening sparked, and bits of hail began to fall as rain slashed across the lawn. Lou wasn't home, and I couldn't leave Josh and Mark alone to search for Sam. I moved back into the house. I thought about calling the police but discounted that idea as being premature.

Sam was smart. Surely he would find shelter at a neighbor's house if he couldn't make it home.

I watched anxiously through the window as high winds and driving rain lashed the house. I was tormented by doubts about my judgment not to call someone to help. Finally, after about an hour the storm passed away. I rushed outside and looked down the road. A great wave of relief washed over me when I saw the two of them walking up the drive, Shepherd leading the way with Sam a few steps behind. Sam smiled and waved.

"Wow, that was some storm," he called.

"It sure was," I agreed. "Where were you?"

Sam pointed back toward Ed and Pat's house. "They weren't home, but we stayed on their carport." Our neighbor's carport was enclosed on three sides. Just as I had hoped, Sam and Shepherd had been safe and dry, although they did get to see nature's fury up close.

Later I gave Shepherd an extra hug. "Thanks for watching over Sam," I said.

For years Sam and Shepherd were a pair. Every day they were together, my boy and his dog.

Seasons pass, and things change. The weathered old farmhouse at the end of our road was torn down, and the horses were taken away. Ultimately, big new houses would be built, and Zoysia grass, shrubs, and flowers would carpet the pastureland. The little town of Helena was growing rapidly as more people discovered its charms. Traffic clogged the main roads during the morning and evening rush hours. Finding a parking space outside the post office was often difficult, and lines frequently formed inside. Helena built a modern library and a municipal building. A developer put in a new shopping area. Old Town was being renovated, and many new subdivisions were under construction. Behind our property, bulldozers cleared the wooded hills on the other side of the valley to make way for new roads and houses.

Shepherd continued his worrisome habit of cruising his former neighborhood. This always concerned us, especially when Helena began to more strictly enforce its leash laws. Many of Shepherd's buddies moved away. Newcomers were not familiar with him. We decided to have him neutered, thinking this would end his urge to wander. But Shepherd had never roamed his old territory for romance as much as for interaction with humans. He had been with us about five-and-a-half years when we received the dreaded phone call. Shepherd was in trouble with the law.

This is the story the police gave us:

A woman in the neighboring subdivision had a small female dog that was in heat. She had put this animal outside in a portable pen. She said that a pack of dogs had crashed through the pen and attacked her pet. The dog wasn't injured, but the pen was destroyed. When she came out of the house screaming, all of the other dogs had scattered. Only Shepherd had hung around to greet the police.

I was angry. I was angry at the woman who had put a dog in heat in a flimsy pen outside and then expected nothing to happen. Why hadn't she had her pet spayed? I was angry at Shepherd. Why couldn't he heed our warnings? I was angry at Lou and myself. We had known something like this was bound to happen. Why hadn't we found a way to prevent it?

I looked at Shepherd as the police officer brought him out to me. He wagged his tail and greeted me with nuzzles and whines. He knew he was in trouble. I was certain he wasn't guilty of gang rape. Surely he had been following the crowd only to see what was happening. Maybe he showed up after it was all over. Maybe it was a big mistake.

"I know Shepherd," the policeman said. "I know he is a good dog."

But the man emphasized that this must never, ever happen again. There could be no more complaints. If there was another incident, we would be held liable and Shepherd's life could be forfeit.

Our options were to put him on an extremely heavy chain or to find him a good home far away from crowded neighborhoods. The decision didn't need a debate. Every member of the family, and most especially Sam, knew that we may as well kill Shepherd as to put him on a chain. We loved him too much for that.

I called the Humane Society and talked to a woman named Patty. I told her I had a huge, friendly German shepherd and explained what had happened.

"He's a beautiful, healthy, smart dog. He's had all of his shots. He's been neutered. He needs a home where he can explore around a bit without bothering anybody. I won't bring him to you unless you are sure you can help us. Under no circumstance will I allow him to be euthanized."

"I'm so glad you called," she said. "My parents live in a rural area of Mississippi. They need a watch dog and asked me to be on the lookout for a good one. It sounds like Shepherd may be just right for them. Why don't you bring him down and let me meet him?"

After taking the children to school the next morning, I loaded Shepherd into the car and headed for the animal shelter. He sat beside me and observed what was happening outside the window, his eyes following the countryside as it flew past. He thought he was on an adventure. Each mile tore another chunk out of my heart.

We stopped at a painted concrete block building with a yard enclosed by chain link fencing. Shepherd and I got out of the car and walked over the gravel parking area, then up a few steps into the building. We entered a room with a metal desk, some filing cabinets, and a few plastic chairs. I could see cages down a hall, and dogs were barking in the back. The place had a strong animal odor, overlaid with an equally strong smell of Pine-Sol. A smiling woman, dressed in jeans and T-shirt, hustled forward to greet us.

"Hi, I'm Patty. This must be Shepherd. Oh, he's gorgeous! What a special dog you are," she gushed as she stroked him and scratched behind his ears. He ate it up, politely raising his paw to shake her hand and wagging his tail. We talked some more. She assured me that he would be well cared for and loved. She attached a rope to his collar, and it was time for me to leave. I knelt down and hugged him, rubbing the sides of his face and sinking my hands into the thick fur around his neck. Shepherd gazed into my eyes, and in that instant he knew what was happening. When I stood up, he lunged after me and began to howl. I swiftly turned and hurried out the door without looking back. I jumped into my car and then sped down the road, weeping all the way home.

After Shepherd left us, Sam began to lose interest in exploring the woods. Oh, he would go out there sometimes, but it wasn't like the old days. He would soon be eleven years old, so maybe he was just growing up, becoming interested in other things.

Shepherd never made it to Mississippi. Patty was carrying him to her parents when she stopped at her sister's home. Her sister lived with her husband and three children out in the country west of Montgomery, Alabama. They didn't know they needed a new dog, but the moment they saw Shepherd, he became a member of their family. The children wrapped their arms around this great and noble beast and cried, "Can we keep him?"

Who could say no?

CHAPTER FIVE

SPOT-SPIKE

I was working in the laundry room one summer day in 1989 when Lou and the boys passed me on the way out the back door.

"I'm taking the guys to the pet shop," Lou announced.

My alarm bells went off. "We don't need another pet," I warned.

"Oh, we're not going to buy anything. We're just going to look, just something to do."

"Uh-huh. Right." Brave man. Three little boys—ages eight, seven, and three—loose in the pet store. What a relaxing way to spend the morning. "Just remember," I called after them, "if you buy anything, I'm not taking care of it."

I was still feeling remorse over our last purchase from the pet store. Lou and company had brought home a cute gerbil a few months before, and his tragic demise had been my fault.

The gerbil had his own cage, complete with an exercise wheel. It was fun to watch him running inside the wheel, racing away, going nowhere. The boys liked to take him out of the cage and play with him. He was a sweet creature, and he had a lot of charm for a rodent. He had big eyes, a chubby little body, and a furry tail. Gerbils rarely bite and are safe to handle. He adored attention. If you held him in your hand, he would sit up on his haunches and wiggle his whiskers as if he were talking to you.

Taking care of the gerbil wasn't difficult. I fed him gerbil food that came in a sack at the grocery store, gave him water, and cleaned his cage whenever necessary. Taking care of my husband and boys and dogs was much more demanding. Caring for the gerbil was just an afterthought.

One pleasant day I decided to take the gerbil's cage outside to clean it. There was a picnic table on the patio, and I thought it would be a good idea to let the gerbil run around on the table top while I worked on the cage. Gerbils will not jump off a ledge, so there was no danger of escape. I dumped the cedar shavings out of the bottom of the cage and replaced them with new ones. Shepherd was still with us at the time, and I had wiped clean the glass sides of the cage, inside and out, and was filling the water dispenser with fresh water when I saw him coming up out of the valley. The gerbil was still exploring the table top, running from side to side, poking his head over the edge and sniffing about.

"Little gerbil, it's time for you to get back inside your cage," I said as I scooped him up into my hands.

At that moment Shepherd saw the gerbil and, giving a mighty WOOF, came bounding toward us. In the next horrifying instant, the panic-stricken gerbil vaulted out of my hands and landed directly inside the wide open mouth of Shepherd, who swallowed him with one satisfied gulp.

The boys gave me disbelieving and dirty looks when I told them what had happened, and consequently I determined that I would not be involved with the care of any future pets.

Some time after I had finished my work in the laundry room, I heard Lou and the boys returning from the pet store. Three excited voices were talking all at once, saying something about a lizard, and Lou gave me a sheepish look as he carried a glass cage into the house.

"You bought a lizard?" I was incredulous. There were hundreds of lizards for the taking outside in the yard, and, as a matter of fact, a number of them had stayed with us as captive guests.

"This one is special."

"He's a tokay gecko..."

"From Southeast Asia!"

"People there keep them in their homes to kill bugs."

"We got a good buy."

"He's real pretty."

"Look!"

I looked. The cage was a lot like a ten gallon fish tank, except that it had a screened lid on top. A lizard about six inches long lay on the bottom of the cage. The creature was bluish-gray with bright orange bumps all over it. It looked like it had some dreadful skin disease.

"That's an interesting lizard," I admitted.

"We got a heat rock and everything!" The boys began pulling supplies out of a sack.

I watched as Lou set up the new lizard home on my laundry room table. Would my life have been different if we'd had girls? Would my table be covered with delicate netting and shiny sequins to make ballet tutus? Would Lou be returning from the store with a pretty porcelain tea set or pink stuffed bunny? Perhaps.

One of the boys brought in a big chunk of wood and some rocks to put in the bottom of the cage so the gecko would have a more natural environment. The heat rock with its electrical cord was settled amidst the other rocks so the lizard could keep its cold-blooded heart warm.

"Let's call him Spot, because he has spots," Mark suggested.

"No, that's a wimpy name," Sam objected.

"I think we should name him Spike," Josh said.

"Yeah, Spike. That's a good name." Sam agreed with Josh.

Mark protested. "Those are spots, not spikes!"

"Well, Spike's a better name than Spot!"

I could see this conversation was headed for battle, so I offered a diplomatic solution. "Why don't we call him Spot-Spike?" I asked.

Josh nodded his head. "That's cool."

Everyone smiled at this ridiculous name, and it was agreed. In reality, as the years went by, Spot-Spike came to be known simply as "the lizard."

I looked at the creature, and it barked at me.

"Is this thing dangerous?" I asked.

"Oh, no. He won't hurt." Sam reached into the tank and wiggled his finger in front of Spot-Spike's face, whereupon the lizard immediately lurched forward and latched onto the tip of Sam's finger.

"Ow! Let go...ouch...he won't let go." Sam tried to pull his finger out of the critter's jaws, but we quickly discovered a basic fact about geckos: once one has latched onto its prey, it never lets go. Fortunately, its teeth weren't extremely sharp, though it did manage to squeeze a small amount of blood from Sam's finger. As the moments passed, I was becoming concerned.

Lou picked up the lizard and tried to pry its mouth open. No luck. "We've got to wedge something between its jaw and Sam's finger."

I handed him a screwdriver. "Try this."

Lou cautiously pushed the tip of the screwdriver into the corner of the lizard's mouth and slid it forward toward Sam's finger. Meanwhile, Sam was grimacing but trying mightily to be brave. At last the lizard's mouth loosened a little, and Sam's finger tip slipped out. We all heaved a sigh of relief, and Lou plopped the creature back into its cage. Spot-Spike probably was as thankful as we were, as he must have realized that Sam was much too big to swallow. Sam's finger didn't look too bad. I cleaned it and put some antibiotic cream on it, and I hoped my son would not develop some deadly reptilian disease. Sam eyed the gecko with new respect.

"Now we know he bites," I said.

"Yeah, don't ever wiggle your finger in front of his face," Sam agreed.

This incident did not discourage the boys from handling Spot-Spike, however, and I often found them sitting in front of the television with the lizard draped over a knee or shoulder. The important thing was to pick him up only if he had been fed first. Years later a pet store owner told me that geckos were known to have mean temperaments, and he was surprised that our lizard allowed himself to be held at all.

That first day, after we had returned Spot-Spike to his cage and doctored Sam's finger, I asked an important question. A nagging suspicion had been growing in my mind.

"What does it eat?"

No one answered at first. I regarded my family as they exchanged looks. "Tell me it eats fruits and vegetables," I said hopefully.

"It eats insects," Lou finally admitted.

"Dead, dehydrated ones you can buy at the pet store?"

"Live ones, but don't worry. We'll catch them. There's lots of insects outside. It won't be a problem at all."

"Well, that's good to know, because if you guys don't feed this lizard, he will die. I am not catching insects for this creature."

To prove their point, the boys got a jar and left the house in search of Spot-Spike's dinner. About thirty minutes later they returned triumphantly with an unfortunate grasshopper.

"I feel sorry for the grasshopper," I said as Sam dropped it into the cage.

"Oh, Mom, it's the food chain."

We watched with morbid fascination. The lizard was lying motionless but quickly raised his head when the grasshopper moved into his visual field. Spot-Spike tensed for a moment, focusing on the insect, then struck with lightning speed. The lizard took his time as he savored the tasty meal. At first the bug's legs hung partially out of the lizard's mouth. Then gradually the gecko pulled the grasshopper deeper into his gullet until at last the legs disappeared.

After he had swallowed the insect, Spot-Spike smacked his mouth several times and stretched his lips backwards into in a wide grin.

"Look at that," I said. This may have been the beginning of feelings I eventually felt for the gecko. "I didn't know lizards could smile."

Licking his chops, Spot-Spike smacked his mouth again. It must have been a delicious grasshopper.

Throughout the summer the boys were constantly on the lookout for lizard food. It was sometimes a challenge. There was an abundant supply of insects outside the house, but they weren't always easy to catch. A person has to have a sharp eye, patience, and a quick hand to catch a grasshopper or cricket. One Sunday morning Josh was standing next to me during church service when he held up his tightly closed fist.

"I've got a grasshopper in here," he whispered.

"You what?"

"A grasshopper. For the lizard. What should I do with it?"

All around me worshippers were singing. The deep and commanding voice of Addison Hitchcock, the song leader, rose up over the congregation, pulling our voices with him, up toward Heaven in praise of the Almighty. Addison was a big man with a majestic voice. Every church needs a singer like Addison.

"I can't believe you brought that thing in here," I whispered furiously back at my son.

"It was in the doorway."

I shuddered as I envisioned what would happen to our proper Presbyterian service if the grasshopper escaped and launched itself across the pews. I reached down for my belongings as the hymn ended and the congregation returned to their seats. I found an envelope in my purse and opened it.

"Put it in here."

The transfer from Josh's hand to envelope was made without incident, and the rest of the service proceeded smoothly. When we got home, the grasshopper gratefully climbed out of the tight confines of the envelope, only to find himself recaptured and quickly dropped into the glass cage, where he became lizard lunch. It was a bad ending for a grasshopper who started his day in church.

Predictably, on a summer morning when I was in the garden pulling weeds, a movement in front of my hands caught my eyes. A fat, dark brown cricket was resting atop the mulch, not six inches from my fingertips. I could catch it easily. I wasn't squeamish. I'm a nurse, a gardener, and the mother of three boys. I had abandoned squeamish sensibilities long ago, but hadn't I promised never to catch insects for this critter? However, the boys weren't here, and I knew Spot-Spike would enjoy the cricket. I made my decision, and in an instant I caught the insect. From that day onward I was always watching out for bugs, and soon I was proficient at capturing them. It became just another part of taking care of my family. To this day, even though Spot-Spike passed on many years ago, if I see a grasshopper or cricket, I still have a little urge to reach out and grab it.

Spot-Spike was a popular attraction. Guests always wanted to see him, and relatives who called to catch up on the health and activities of various members of the family usually would also ask how the lizard was doing. My boys sometimes drew other people into the search for lizard food. Once, a contractor and his crew of workers, who were being paid by the hour, turned over a long board behind the house and discovered a large colony of crickets. Mark had introduced Spot-Spike to the contractor, so the man knew all about the lizard.

"Get me a jar," he called.

Soon all the workers were on their hands and knees catching crickets. How nice. That was enough crickets to feed the lizard for several weeks. Then I remembered how much I was paying these guys to catch bugs.

A friend told Lou about a local bait shop that carried live crickets. This was an inexpensive, easy alternative to hand-caught insects when the supply in our yard ran low or we all were too busy with other activities to catch insects. A couple of dollars would buy a whole month's supply. Spot-Spike wasn't greedy. He would eat just enough to satisfy himself, and then the rest of the crickets were free to roam the cage until he became hungry again.

At first I felt sorry for the crickets. I fondly remembered the character Jiminy Cricket from Walt Disney's animated film, *Pinocchio*. And I had always heard that crickets were good luck, so my tender heart had feelings of regret when we dropped the first ones into the cage with the lizard.

Those feelings did not last long. Crickets are horrid creatures. To my disgust, I soon discovered that they are cannibals. After that, I was happy to add them to the food chain.

Spot-Spike was a little choosy about what he would eat. We once substituted mealworms when the bait shop was out of crickets. These tawny, worm-like creatures are the larvae of mealworm beetles. Most geckos love mealworms. Our lizard was intrigued but refused to eat the new offering. He watched the mealworms as they crawled around his cage, tilting his head to one side, then the other, as he considered them. Finally, he gave one of the mealworms a tentative touch of the tongue. He then proceeded to lick the creature from end to end, as though giving it a bath. Those wormy critters wiggled in front of his mouth and even climbed up onto his snout, and still he refused to bite. Never once in his long life, regardless of how hungry he was, did Spot-Spike eat anything that resembled a worm.

Moths, on the other hand, were a favorite delicacy. On warm summer nights moths congregated around the mercury light on the side of our house, and they were easy to catch in a butterfly net. Spot-Spike always seemed happy to get a moth as a side dish to his usual grasshopper or cricket. One evening Josh accompanied Lou to the grocery store, and he hand-caught a moth outside the store and brought it home.

"Come see what I have!" He opened his hands.

"Wow! Look at that…"

We all gathered around and gawped at the largest moth we had ever seen. As it lay in Josh's open hands, the wings spread out to completely cover both his palms, with a span of at least five to six inches. It made no effort to escape.

"It's for the lizard," Josh stated.

I looked at the creature. It had a velvety white body and luminescent, pale green wings. It was beautiful. "I've never seen anything like that. Are you sure we should feed it to the lizard? What if it's some sort of endangered species?"

I later did some research and learned that the creature was a luna moth, also known as the American moon moth. It is not on any endangered species list, but it is threatened in some areas by urban pollution, loss of habitat, and insecticides. Luna moths are not seen very often, because they live only about a week after emerging from their cocoons. Their sole purpose as an adult moth is to mate and produce eggs. They do not feed at all during their short lives—in fact, they have no mouths—and they perish soon after mating.

"It's dying anyway. That's how I was able to catch it. It was just flopping around."

Although I still had some doubts, I agreed to feed it to Spot-Spike. Josh dropped the moth into the cage. At first the gecko remained motionless. But when the moth spread its huge wings, the lizard immediately raised his head and crept forward, then halted, alert and poised to attack. The moth flopped once, and the lizard struck.

The awful thing was that the moth was way too big for Spot-Spike's mouth. The body of the moth was inside his mouth, but a great wing hung out each side. The moth was still alive in there, and it began to flap its wings. The gecko looked like a flying dragon, getting ready for takeoff.

"Oh, no! He's going to choke."

"I think he can manage it," Lou said.

We watched as agonizingly slowly one wing, then the other, disappeared into the lizard's mouth. At last, after far too many long minutes, the moth was successfully swallowed.

Spot-Spike wiped his mouth with his tongue and gave a great smile of satisfaction.

But I have never forgotten the look of those flapping wings, and I have regretted it ever since. I think that was one moth that should have died of natural causes.

Once in a while Spot-Spike would escape from his cage. If the wire screen lid was not firmly pushed into place, sometimes a small crack at the corner would offer a route to the free world. The first time this happened, I was frantic. Even if people in Southeast Asia allow geckos to roam freely inside their homes, I didn't want one wandering my halls, exploring dark corners while we were sleeping. Geckos are primarily nocturnal, and I didn't like the idea of waking up in the middle of the night with a lizard latched onto one of my toes. By then we had moved Spot-Spike's cage from the laundry room to Sam's bedroom, so we began searching there. We soon found the lizard resting nonchalantly on the wall behind a bookcase. I was extremely relieved.

Josh had a friend named Jeff who admired our gecko. Jeff talked his mother into purchasing a gecko for his very own. All was well for a few weeks, but then Jeff's lizard escaped. Despite a house-wide search, they did not find the critter. Jeff's family finally gave up the search, assuming that somehow their lizard had found its way outside.

Nearly a year passed. Then one fine day Jeff's mother saw a movement behind the refrigerator. It was the gecko, very much alive and well nourished. I don't suppose they had any bugs in their kitchen that year.

Whenever Spot-Spike would get loose, we usually located him without too much searching. Most often we found him hanging out on the wall inside the closet. Geckos can climb walls and even move across ceilings, because their rounded toes are covered with hundreds of tiny hairs that enable them to adhere to surfaces. They do this by using the electrostatic properties of something called van der Waals forces. NASA scientists, inspired by what they learned from the gecko, have used van der Waals forces to develop gripper technology that is now used by astronauts on the International Space Station, as well as by many manufacturing facilities on Earth.

Spot-Spike never traveled far. Then one year he vanished, just a few weeks before Christmas. Despite a search throughout the house, we could not find him. We searched every wall, every closet, behind every piece of furniture. I remembered Jeff's lizard and had hopes that he would turn up. The boys would come home from school each day and ask if I had found the lizard. I regularly checked behind the refrigerator, but as the weeks passed I began to think that our lizard was gone for good.

Before bedtime we always had "hug and prayer time" with the boys, and a few nights before Christmas, Mark had a special request.

"Dear God, please let our lizard come home for Christmas," he prayed.

"Amen," I said.

Christmas Eve night Mark was in the boys' bathroom when he noticed something peculiar about the wall. There was a bulge under the wallpaper, and it was moving.

"Mom! Mom!" he shouted. "Come here! I found the lizard!"

I had previously noted areas where the wallpaper was coming loose and had tried to glue it. My workmanship must not have been very good, because Spot-Spike had found a loose seam and was crawling around between the wallpaper and the wall. He was fat and happy. We returned the lizard to his cage, and I was thankful that God was great enough to care about little things that were important to the heart of a small boy.

Spot-Spike lived with us about a dozen years, a long time for a tokay gecko. During those years, Sam, Josh, and Mark grew into teenagers with varied interests. There were model rockets, girls, guitars, art lessons, and automobiles. There were automobile wrecks. Mark developed diabetes at age seven years, nine months—the exact age Sam had been when he was stricken. We sucked up our guts and doubled our supply of insulin and syringes. We went to soccer games, football games, and swim meets. We collected coins and comic books. We went through three different Nintendo game systems. We bought our first computer. There were camping trips with the Boy Scouts, hikes along the Appalachian Trail, and family holidays at the beach. We all traveled to Arizona one year and explored that arid and beautiful country, which was so alien to the lush, green land of Alabama. Lou made a point to treat each boy to a special father/son vacation. He took Josh to the San Diego Zoo, and he and Sam went on a fishing trip in the Florida Keys. Mark spent a week at Space Camp in Huntsville, and he sailed on a schooner around the Bahamas. Sam and Josh took a trip with their older cousin Ross to England and Scotland. And always there were school projects and homework. The flow of life continued its winding course. Sometimes when we were settled in and comfortable with the journey, confident that we knew just where we were heading, an unexpected turn would force us into some bewildering and unwelcome place, and choppy waves would threaten to overwhelm us. But we remained family, and we worked hard to get out of the turbulent spots, until at last we could ease back and relax for a while.

And through all those years, we were catching bugs for the lizard.

When he died, I buried Spot-Spike in the garden near flowering shrubs and dogwood trees. Josh pronounced a perfect eulogy. It was simple and yet said it all:

"He was a good lizard."

CHAPTER SIX

SOMETHING FISHY

Lou brought with him into our marriage a plecostomus catfish, commonly called a pleco. Prior to meeting Mozart, I would not have considered a fish a pet. After all, you can't "pet" a fish! At best, I thought of Lou's fish tank as a hobby. About six inches long, Mozart was unbelievably ugly, with mud-colored spotted scales, lumpy eyes, and whiskers across his snout. He was a bottom feeder with an underslung suckermouth. He functioned as the fish tank's janitor, pulling up stuff from the bottom of the tank like a vacuum cleaner. He would also attach his round mouth to the sides of the fish tank, and we could get a good view of the inside of his gullet as he rasped off algae, of which he was particularly fond. We enjoyed his weirdness. He was peaceful toward other fish, and he was fun to watch. This character won me over, and soon I was attaching distinctive pet-like qualities to him. He lived about ten years, and he was one of my favorites.

Fish are relatively easy-care pets. Lou had maintained a fish tank since childhood, and shortly after we married we purchased a thirty-gallon setup. All you have to do for fish is feed them and occasionally clean their tank. If you have the right kind of equipment—a heater to keep the water at the appropriate temperature and a good filter to keep the water from getting too gunky—the work is minimal. This is easy for me to say, since I personally never cleaned the tank. Every month or so Lou spent part of an afternoon cleaning the inside of the glass, replacing filters, and changing out part of the water. He never complained about the responsibility.

For the most part, fish are non-stressful and less expensive than most other pets. They don't eat siding off the house, dig holes in the yard, or create problems with the neighbors. Watching them can lower blood pressure and soothe the soul. I sometimes would pause by the fish tank on my way to perform some important duty—then twenty minutes later I would pull myself out of it, suddenly realizing I had been unconsciously gazing at the fish as they ever-so-subtly hypnotized me with their flowing tails and shimmering bodies. Doctors' and dentists' offices sometimes contain fish tanks, and I wondered if they were put there in order to psychologically anesthetize the patients in preparation for upcoming treatments.

Many fish are beautiful, with jewel tone colors and gorgeous tails and fins. I was surprised to learn that they can have interesting personalities. They don't demand a lot of emotional investment, but we became quite attached to some of them, especially those who, like Mozart, had a lot of character.

I was particularly fond of our black ghost knife fish. This was a stunning, strange creature with a slender, matte black body shaped like a knife. I was enthralled by its movements—it undulated gracefully and quickly through the water with ribbon-like motions, flowing effortlessly through its environment rather than cutting through the water as most fish do.

It possessed an eccentric look. Its face reminded me of a sleek dog, with a canine-like jaw line, an intelligent expression, and a creamy stripe down the center of its nose. This unusual fish got its name from the tribal lore of some South American Indians who, impressed with the creature's appearance, applied spiritual qualities to it. They believed each black ghost held the soul of a departed human. Harming one was strictly taboo. Watching the black ghost, it was easy to understand how they developed this philosophy.

Our black ghost was a friendly fish who frequently came up to the side of the tank to visit with me. The elegant creature liked to eat out my hand. Sometimes I would push my face against the side of the tank and stare at him, and he would stare back, his face right in front of my eyes, seemingly as curious as I was. Do fish have thought processes? I was sure that in some way our black ghost did, and I wondered what the creature was thinking.

In the wild, black ghosts can grow to nearly two feet long. Our knife fish had no hope of growing that large in our thirty gallon tank. Many years later, I read that a black ghost should be put in nothing smaller than a hundred gallon tank! Our black ghost had grown to about eight inches long when it prematurely died after suffering a drug reaction to a medication Lou used to treat some other fish.

Fish can get sick with diseases such as ick, dropsy, and tail rot. The pet store carried an assortment of antibiotics and anti-fungal treatments, and occasionally we had to use them. There are specialized fish veterinarians, but I never heard of one in our area, so we had to rely on scanty information in a fish book to diagnose and decide on which treatment to use. Sometimes we were successful, and sometimes not.

Many fish ailments are contagious, and one sick fish can wipe out an entire tank. Buying a new fish could be a little risky, and it was not a bad idea to treat the tank preventatively with an antibacterial agent when introducing a newcomer. But we sorrowfully learned that tank treatment could also be dangerous, because fish can have bad reactions to medications, just like humans.

Lou and I were both saddened when our black ghost died. These fascinating fish are not easy to find, and large ones can be expensive. So some years later when I came across a small one in an aquarium shop, I eagerly bought it. This black ghost was just as beautiful as the first one, but it had a completely different disposition. The second black ghost was shy and stayed hidden behind rocks most of the day. It never came to the side of the tank to interact with me. Although it lived for nearly a decade, we caught only fleeting glimpses of it, and I was never able to get it to take food directly from my hand. I was amazed that two fish of the same species could have completely different temperaments, just as some people are outgoing while others are timid. I pondered the idea that all creatures have individual characteristics and personalities. Would this apply to something like an ant or a worm? It doesn't seem likely, but there are a lot of things we humans don't know—and don't know that we don't know!

We had become dependent on Mozart, our pleco catfish, to help keep the fish tank clean. After he died, a quick hunt of local fish shops failed to find another pleco. Algae began building up on the sides of the tank, so Lou searched for another kind of algae eater.

One day he came home with a fire-bellied newt. The helper at the fish store told him that the newt was a bottom feeder/algae eater, as Mozart had been. This creature looked like some kind of primordial lizard, a relic from the days of the dinosaurs. The fire-bellied newt was appropriately named. His upper body was dull reddish-brown, but brilliant, lava-colored splotches covered his underside.

We called the newest member of our tank community Sir Isaac Newton. But he never lived up to his distinguished title, for he turned out to be exceptionally dim-witted. I don't know that he was born that way. I'm afraid his mental slowness resulted from our own unintentional neglect. He seemed fine when we first put him in the tank, but as time passed he became lethargic and began to lose weight. I was concerned that he may have brought some exotic disease with him, as sometimes other new members of the aquarium community had done. After several weeks he was almost skeletal.

"You know," I said to Lou, "I haven't seen this newt eat anything since we got him. Are you sure he's an algae eater?"

"That's what I was told."

I decided to do a little research—something we should have done before buying any fish (or any pet!). Fish purchases were often impromptu acquisitions, and this experience taught us that a teenager hired to help around an aquarium shop may not be the best source of information. Reading through a fish book, I discovered that our newt didn't eat plants at all—he was a meat eater! He needed food such as brine shrimp and blood worms. He couldn't eat algae or any of the flake food we routinely fed to the tropical fish that inhabited the aquarium with him. We had nearly starved the creature to death.

We purchased some brine shrimp and put them in the tank. Unfortunately, Sir Isaac Newton was so weak that he was unable to feed. He lay on the bottom of the tank, disinterested in the food floating about his head. I stuck my hand into the fish tank and grabbed a clump of the tiny shrimp pieces. I waved them in front of the newt's face, tempting him. No luck. I repeatedly touched his mouth with the shrimp. When at last his mouth opened a bit, I stuffed in the food. But the newt made no effort to swallow, and globs of shrimp hung out the sides of his mouth. I continued to gently tickle his mouth, until at last the newt closed his mouth around the food and slowly swallowed. I repeated the maneuver, and this time he took the shrimp a little more quickly. Finally!

He was going to be OK. I hand-fed him every day, and gradually he began to regain weight and to become more active. Whenever he saw me, he would eagerly come to the side of the tank and wait expectantly for his food, like a puppy prancing in anticipation. He eventually put on so much weight that his belly became disproportionately round and his little lizard legs stuck out like sausages. He lumbered around the tank, planting his feet as if he were a great dinosaur, and I imagined the earth quaking with each step. I changed his name from Sir Isaac Newton to Fatboy.

Fatboy died at age fifteen years, outliving all of his original co-inhabitants of the tank. The problem with Fatboy was that he never learned to feed himself. The smelliest, meatiest morsel could be directly in front of him, and he would stare stupidly at it until I reached down and offered it to him with my fingers. Lou says I spoiled him. I tried a few times to be tough in an effort to make Fatboy feed himself, but I never succeeded. As soon as he began to look hungry—and he could look very pitiful for an amphibian, gazing up at me and begging—I would relent and feed it to him. I still felt guilty about how he got into this predicament.

Fatboy was the most docile creature we ever had in the tank. Our second black ghost and he became companions. They were about the same size, and they often rested together amidst the rocks. When I would feed Fatboy, the black ghost had the custom of coming up to feed on the stuff hanging out of the newt's mouth, since the newt was always slow about taking the food completely into his mouth and swallowing it. I was astonished that Fatboy never complained and seemed wholly content to share his food.

One year we purchased a pair of parrotfish. These were round, shimmering orange beauties with flowing fins and tails. They had cute, bow-shaped mouths that were always slightly open. We realized they were male and female when we noticed them kissing each other. They were locking lips, smooching with their mouths, just like humans. Not long afterwards, the female laid about a thousand eggs, but conditions in the tank weren't favorable and none of the eggs produced any fish. Other inhabitants of the tank eventually ate up all the eggs.

The parrotfish had enormous appetites. Each one was the aquatic equivalent of a Labrador retriever. I never saw them refuse food. If given enough, they probably would have eaten until they exploded. They must have noticed how the black ghost ate out of Fatboy's mouth, because they soon began to do the same. This was too much, even for mild-mannered Fatboy. One day I watched as he turned around and grabbed hold of a raider's flowing tail and then clung to it as the parrotfish rapidly retreated to the other side of the tank, towing Fatboy all the way.

"Good for you, Fatboy! You stick up for yourself!"

Fatboy's dull little teeth didn't harm the fish, and I never saw him do it again. Afterwards, I made sure the parrotfish had plenty of their own food before I reached down to give Fatboy his meal.

Most of the fish we have owned came from pet stores. But when he was young, Sam would sometimes come home with various types of aquatic life from the nearby lake at Joe Tucker Park. We watched a couple of little tadpoles develop into frogs in our tank. We then captured the little frogs and took them back to the park.

Sam and Lou once came in from a fishing trip with a tiny bream swimming in a bucket. Sam had netted it and wanted to put it in the aquarium. Lou thought it was a great idea. Bream are good to eat. Their white meat is sweet and flaky and is considered one of the tastiest freshwater fishes. I wondered if Lou planned to raise the bream until it was mature, then fry it up for supper one day. The bream flourished in our tank, but trouble arose when it began to eat the other fish. Lou and Sam quickly netted it and returned it to the lake, where it legitimately faced the possibility of becoming someone's meal.

The rule in our fish community was that you had to get along. Rarely, we purchased fish that turned out to be bullies, and we ended up taking them back to the store or finding them other homes. That's what happened with a Siamese fighting fish I once bought. Its name was a tip-off, and I should have known better. After only one day, I sheepishly returned it to the aquarium shop. The salesperson rolled his eyes and shook his head, but he did take the fish back, though he refused to refund my money. The fish had cost just a couple of dollars, and I didn't feel like debating. I was glad to get it off my hands and hoped the next purchaser would provide a better home.

We once had a creature that committed suicide. The sad tale began when Lou and the boys returned from one of their trips to the pet store with a Jamaican shrimp. This was a freshwater shrimp that looked much like the saltwater kind we eat, but of course it still had all of its legs, antennae, and pincers. I think it may have been a relative to the crawdads that we found in our local creeks. At the time, we had some angel fish, as well as Fatboy and the second black ghost.

The Jamaican shrimp immediately began terrorizing the other inhabitants of the aquarium, grabbing at fins and chasing the others away. It strutted around the tank while Fatboy and the black ghost and all the angel fish hid behind rocks. I watched its display of bad behavior and hoped that after a few days it would settle down and become more sociable.

That did not happen. The next day the Jamaican shrimp was still in a foul mood as it scrambled over the rocks and glared down at the occupants cowering in the crevices. This bully hated its new home. It began hitting the sides of the tank with its pincers, like a prisoner pounding at the bars of his jail cell. I began to think we would have to return it to the pet store.

Then a few days later I looked into the tank, and I was glad to see the angel fish swimming around peacefully and Fatboy clumping along the bottom. At last all seemed well in the aquarium. Then I realized I didn't see the Jamaican shrimp.

I searched behind the rocks. There was the black ghost, but no shrimp. Huh. Maybe Lou had done something with it, like flush it down the toilet. Then I noticed a splotch of water on the shelf that held the tank. There was also a track of moisture on the outside of the aquarium's glass wall. I looked on the hardwood floor. More water, but no shrimp.

I peered closer and saw droplets leading out into the hallway. I followed the trail and looked down the hall. Twelve feet away, at the end of the hallway, I found the dead Jamaican shrimp.

I was astounded that it had been able to get so far. I have since thought about the Jamaican shrimp and wondered about its last moments. In its own way, did it revel in its freedom as it pulled itself over the glass wall, not realizing that the boundaries of the fish tank secured safety and life? Perhaps at first it marveled at the forbidden territory it had entered and fearlessly set out to explore it. Did it realize it was in trouble as it crawled along the path to its destruction? Did it suffer before the gasses of our atmosphere took its life? Was there panic before the end, or was there only ignorance? I have decided that, to a small degree, Jamaican shrimp may be similar to people, who sometimes ignore boundaries and then find themselves lost to unforeseen and unforgiving consequences.

CHAPTER SEVEN

⹂Tornado

One year Josh and I visited cousin Ross, who lived in New York City. When he showed us his tiny Manhattan apartment, he proudly pointed to a window over the kitchen sink. African violets bloomed in pots on the windowsill. Outside, several trees reached up to his fourth floor apartment from a small plaza below.

Our daily lives may be contained within asphalt and concrete, but it seems we all instinctively want to possess a piece of paradise, however small. If we have a yard, we often start with a tree or some shrubs, but then we may start thinking, maybe some flowers over there, how about another tree...and before we know it, plants have taken over our weekends and our budget. If we have no yard, we may instead fall under the spell of houseplants. And if growing indoor plants doesn't work out because we don't have light-filled windows or because our schedules are too busy or because for some other reason we always kill them, we may succumb to the charms of the fake ones. It's in our genetic make-up. Our bodies are made from elements of the soil—it is part of who we are. We inherently need plants to nourish our spirits. Surely there is hope for the most hardened criminal, if you can put that person in a garden.

After we sold the tree house, I was concerned that we would miss its surrounding greenery and wildlife, but in Helena I found my own little corner of paradise. I was in awe of the towering oak trees that bordered the perimeter of our front lawn. A few of them had been growing since before the Civil War. In addition to oak trees, the forest contained pine, hickory, sycamore, dogwood and redbud trees. Assorted azaleas, beautyberry, wax myrtle, and other shade loving shrubs grew beneath the trees. It was a priceless, park-like setting—a play yard for the children and the dogs, a perfect habitat for many forest creatures, and a visual delight for me. I liked to sit in the living room by the large windows that stretched twelve feet across the front of the house, relaxing as I absorbed the scenery. The seasons changed and the years rolled by in front of those windows.

Spring could begin as early as February and last into May. Each year as the world began to wake from its winter slumber, the palest haze of chartreuse green shoots and leaves began to emerge out of the muted landscape. Then, as if the drowsy land had suddenly responded to an alarm clock, overnight a medley of bright colors burst across the garden in shades of pink, lavender, blue, yellow, and white. Periwinkles and wild violets carpeted the woodland, while daffodils offered up their cheerful cups above the groundcover. Like graceful ladies, dogwoods and redbud trees covered themselves with delicate blossoms, their slender trunks rising amidst billowing skirts of colorful azaleas.

The temperature outside was pleasant, and the atmosphere was suffused with intoxicating smells. Every day I would take a deep breath of spring, inhaling the earthy scent of damp soil, the aroma of newly laid pine straw mulch, the sweet smells of fragrant snowball viburnum and tender roses—fruity smells and pungent smells and grassy smells, along with the exhilarating smell of cool, clean air.

Spring was glorious. Each year it pulled me outside to dig in the soil and to plant, to prune, and to weed. Gentle sunshine filtered through the trees and cast lacy patterns over the woodland floor. Stress flowed away as I worked, and I relished my part in growing the body of the earth. I occasionally would pause, sensing the powerful forces at work around me. All the creatures of the woods were busy making babies and caring for them. Their songs and calls celebrated life, producing an ever-changing symphony of background music, rising and falling as the season played out its dramas.

As summer approached, colors intensified. My yard turned deep green and hot, shot through with the bright pinks and shocking red and orange hues of common, gutsy plants that reveled in the heat and brazenly shouted out to the pollinators, "Come on, let's do it!" Crepe myrtle, butterfly bushes, canna lilies, salvia, marigolds, and zinnias teemed with bees and butterflies. A mist of swarming gnats settled low across the lawn.

Summer also brought an abundance of food. Growing food, preparing food, and eating food have always been important parts of Southern culture, as it is in other cultures over the world, for we are a land of culinary delights. Through the generations, Southern families have gathered around food to connect and to swap stories, sometimes to debate or argue with one another, often interrupting the conversation to say, "Pass the peas, please."

Summertime tables traditionally overflowed with nourishing, stick-to-the-ribs, soul-satisfying fare: potato salad, green beans, juicy sweet corn, fried okra, yellow squash, mashed potatoes, sliced homegrown tomatoes, along with fried chicken or baked ham or a pot roast resting in its own gravy. Sweet, buttery yeast rolls complemented everything else, while we drank tall, frosty glasses of iced tea or zesty, sweet lemonade. For dessert there were Grandma's special chocolate layer cake and big bowls full of homemade ice cream topped with fresh strawberries or peaches, which we all, young and old, shoveled into our mouths. Finally, summer was never complete without ice-cold watermelon—refreshing, sugary, and succulent—to be eaten at any part of a meal or just as a snack.

In the Deep South, all of life's important events are set against a backdrop of food. Whether one is celebrating or lamenting, you always get food. If you are sick, if you have a baby, if you get married, or if someone dies, people bring food. Food does more than fill the stomach. It is a practical thing, but it is also a loving thing. It is an important way people show they care.

Many people envision a garden primarily as a plot of ground to grow food, with neat rows of plants such as beans, peas, potatoes, corn, and tomatoes. When we moved to Helena, the one thing I regretted about my shady yard was the lack of enough sunshine to support a vegetable garden. But I was happy that nearby there were roadside stands brimming with fresh vegetables, as well as baskets of Chilton County peaches and just-picked strawberries and blueberries—all at reasonable prices.

In truth, the food was plentiful and delicious, but I didn't always enjoy summer. Although our property was blessed with ample shade, even the canopy of trees offered little relief during the torpid, sweltering dog days of July and August.

Summer was the time to be lazy. Even our active outdoor dogs napped the days away beneath shrubs in cool depressions they dug in the earth. When the outside world wilted under summer's intense glare, the best thing to do was to retreat into the house to rest in chilly, air-conditioned comfort.

Sometimes, feeling guilty about the jungle growing outside, I would decide to pull a few weeds. But almost immediately after I stepped outside and was engulfed by the suffocating vapors of summer, my clothes would be sticking to my body and I would be gasping for breath. Coming to my senses, I would stumble back into the house, thinking that someday those weeds were going to perish of their own accord. I refused to think about their offspring.

So I would stay inside, crank up the AC, and worry about the power bill later. How did people live in this climate before air conditioning? It was a mystery.

I hoped for rain. I would search the sky throughout the day as the temperature climbed and the air thickened, watching as a gray haze developed on the horizon. On a lucky day, in late afternoon the wind would begin to blow and lightning would flash as billowing, black clouds piled up in the sky and then finally dumped rain over the earth. The storm usually passed quickly. Afterwards, water vapor would rise above the road as the air cooled, however briefly.

Butterflies danced amidst the flowers as summer advanced, and hummingbirds performed amazing aerial maneuvers. In the background, a rhythmic rising and falling chorus of cicadas became so loud that the bugs sounded very much like an invasion of UFOs in an old B-grade sci-fi movie. I have heard cicadas my entire life and hardly pay attention to them, but their high-pitched, powerful buzzing can be quite alarming to someone who is unaccustomed to them.

When the year at last stretched into October, the sun became less fierce and tinted the earth with rich, golden rays. The earth glowed, radiant in mellow tones of buttery yellow, burgundy, and purple. Many plants that had languished in the summer heat finally perked up and began to put out new growth and flowers. Fall gardens featured pansies, asters and mums, zinnias and marigolds. Colorful blooms often continued until the first frosts in November came to nip them down.

We enjoyed being outside again, and the dogs romped with renewed vigor. Now was the time for yard work, though it hardly seemed like work to me. Fall is a good time in the Deep South to transplant and to put in new shrubs and bulbs. In the autumn of our first years in Helena, I dug up lots of azaleas that I thought were in the wrong places and found better locations for them. I bought new ones to add to their number. I planted hundreds of daffodils.

I pulled weeds and sprayed herbicide on the poison oak that sprouted everywhere. Lou hacked at massive vines, thick as a man's wrist, and ripped them out of dogwoods and other trees. He repeatedly battled the kudzu that covered part of the valley and threatened to force its way toward our house. He regularly chopped at a mass of bamboo behind the house to halt its spread into the parking area. And all the English ivy! The original owners of our property loved ivy and had planted a few sprigs here and there. So beautiful—but it had wandered unchecked for many years, and now it was consuming the woods. Lou went out with his machete every year and did what he could to control these invasive plants. I shook my head at the obnoxious vegetation and envisioned a date far into a distant future when the kudzu, the bamboo, and the ivy would overrun our then dilapidated, abandoned house, pushing through broken windows and fighting for supremacy over the roof.

But not yet.

Our land was a paradise only in the imaginations of our minds, but in the coolness of fall we worked hard and dreamed of the beauty that would come with spring.

Then winter would sneak in, usually arriving by Christmas or shortly afterwards. I liked to take these months to rest from gardening, though some days were mild and good for pruning or planting dormant trees. I always looked forward to the arrival of new garden catalogs, an event that brightened winter's dreary, damp days. Winter was a good time to plan, and the colorful catalogues offered tempting inspiration.

I don't like cold weather, so I am glad for our short winters. Yet I have always appreciated the warm, cuddly side of the season. On chilly mornings while the rest of us were still sleeping, Lou often rose early to build a fire in the living room's big stone fireplace. What a wonderful man. When I finally climbed out of bed, I would head toward the warmth of the crackling fire. A working fireplace adds an ambiance to winter that is hard to beat.

We rarely built a fire in our second fireplace, located in the kitchen. That almost always made the place too hot, and we would end up having to open windows to let the heat out. The house would have been cozy without any fire at all, because the man who built our house put radiant heating under all the floors. Nothing feels better to bare feet than preheated floors on a cold morning. But I liked the character of the kitchen fireplace, so I put some logs in it and hung a cast iron pot over them, as if I were planning to cook pioneer style over the flames.

For me, winter is forever imprinted with memories of our first January in Helena, with newborn Mark nestled against my chest as we contentedly basked in the glow from the nearby living room fireplace. The days slipped by while I rocked my baby and watched the panorama outside the room's expanse of windows.

Winter's landscape was subdued, with stark, gray trees and bare shrubs and monotonous swathes of beige grass stretching beyond the house. Nevertheless, the countryside bustled with wildlife even in January. Rabbits frequently used our front walkway to get from one part of the yard to another, and sometimes they would pause in front of the door and look toward the house. I wondered if they could see me peering at them from within.

"They are coming to worship the rabbit god," Lou joked, pointing to our concrete rabbit, which sat at the bottom of the front steps. The rabbit had been a Christmas gift to me from Lou. To this day it remains in the same spot, though it now displays a patina of age with moss-filled cracks in one ear, as well as in a few other places.

I watched as a couple of cardinals flitted in and out of the big forsythia bush on the other side of the driveway, the male's red plumage providing a bright spot in January's drab vista. I also liked to observe the squirrels who boldly hopped into the stone planter below the windows and dug for nuts they had previously hidden. Contented, I rocked my baby as each day slipped toward night while I admired the rosy blush of the sunset visible through the dark lacework of my beloved trees.

Lasting about two fitful months, winter's grip is never very secure. Semi-tropical Alabama is caught between the torrid tropical climate below us and the more temperate regions above us, and the two environments often clash over the state. A lot of winter days are cold and sleety, but our weather can be an atmospheric rollercoaster ride with temperatures rapidly rising and plunging. I was wearing summer shorts one warm December day, then a few mornings later we were all digging for our coats and long underwear as the temperature plummeted to four degrees Fahrenheit.

We experienced unusually mild weather in January 1990, with temperatures hovering in the seventies. By February the daffodils were in full bloom and many other plants had started their spring growth. But winter still had a punch of icy Canadian air to deliver. In the early hours of February tenth, this frosty air collided with warm, moist air coming up from the Gulf of Mexico, thus generating the perfect conditions for volatile, dangerous weather.

Before I went to bed on the ninth, I paid scarce attention to the local weather report on the ten o'clock news. The meteorologist mentioned the possibility of severe thunderstorms, but all was calm outside. Lou and I tucked the children into their beds and then soon settled under our own covers and drifted to sleep. Shepherd rested near the front steps, while Susie lay inside the dog yard. Spot-Spike had wrapped himself around the heat rock inside his glass cage. All was well in our secure and comfortable world.

At two-twenty-five a.m., the bedside telephone jangled once, waking both of us, and then went silent. As I struggled to conscious-ness, I glanced at the florescent hands of the small alarm clock. Puzzled, I listened for a moment. Something was happening. A loud, clattering noise sounded like gravel hitting the side of the house. Later, I realized that the single ring of the telephone was due to the telephone line being struck by lightning and that the gravel sound was caused by hail.

"There's a storm," Lou said as he got out of the bed and headed toward the other side of the house where the children were sleeping.

I sat up. The wind was howling ominously.

"I think it's a tornado," I said, yet doubtful that it could really be so.

I followed Lou. As I passed through the living room, an unbelievable scene from a disaster movie was playing outside the windows. Booming thunder reverberated continuously, and my big oak trees, backlit by the scintillating strobe of lightning flashes, were bending toward the house. The tops of those giant trees were halfway to the ground. And an awful roar was coming from behind the trees.

"Lou, it is a tornado! Get the children!"

By the time I reached the hallway outside the boys' bedrooms, Lou already had Sam and Josh huddled there under blankets. He left them with me and went to get Mark. He quickly scooped our youngest son out of his bed and joined the rest of us in the hall.

We don't have a basement. The hallway, in the center of the house and away from windows, was the safest place to be. As Lou and I covered the children's bodies with our own, the thought crossed my mind that we could die that night.

Stay calm. Stay calm. Stay calm, I told myself. But my heart was battering against my chest wall, and I could barely breathe.

"Oh, God, please protect us."

Things began to pound the house. We felt a monstrous thump, then another and another, as the relentless wind blasted our home.

"That's the trees," Lou said. "They're falling on the house."

The earth literally shook beneath the tornado as it assaulted the landscape and headed our way. The entire house began to vibrate as the sucking whirlwind grabbed hold of us like an angry giant. We heard wood splintering, things ripping. Throughout the house, our aluminum blinds were rattling, although all the windows were closed.

A moment later it was over. Less than five minutes had passed since the jangle of the telephone had wakened us. We were safe. The house was still standing, though we weren't sure what kind of damage we had sustained.

"What about the neighbors?"

I went to the living room and looked out the windows, which remarkably were unbroken. I peered through a screen of tree trunks that were leaning against the front of our house. The thunderstorm continued to rage outside, and the night sky was still pulsing with bursts of vivid lightning. The eerie, purplish light enabled me to see down the road, and in the distance I saw the house belonging to Ed and Pat. It looked OK. I went to the kitchen and looked out the glass door. Betty's house, located through the woods to the side of us, was also still standing.

"It looks like the neighbors are all right," I told Lou, who was gathering flashlights.

"How about the dogs?"

I opened the back door. Susie was standing there on the breezeway between the house and Lou's office. She was panting, and her eyes were bright. She wagged her tail as she greeted me. I petted her and let her know I was very glad to see her too.

"It looks like the fence is gone, because Susie is out of the dog yard. She's fine. I don't see Shepherd."

"Well, there's not much we can do till morning."

Lou and I went back through the house to the boys, who remained in the hallway, still groggy with sleep, more or less aware of what had happened. Popping noises were coming from the ceiling, and we worried that the roof might collapse.

"What should we do?" I asked.

"Lets put the guys in our bed," Lou suggested.

So we gathered them up and headed for our bedroom. I wrinkled my nose. A strong, stringent odor permeated the air.

"What's that smell?" I asked.

"Pine resin. From all the broken pine trees."

Or broken house, I thought, remembering that our house is built from pine lumber. We had just settled the boys into our bed when the ceiling above us began to split, and a stream of water poured down onto the middle of the bed.

"Uh, oh. I guess we better get out of here. Lets go to Sam and Josh's room."

We hustled back to the other side of the house, and grave, cracking noises continued. The five of us settled uneasily into the one room, some of us on the two twin beds, the rest of us on the floor. I looked up at the big beams that crossed the ceiling. I had always liked those beams.

"You don't think the beams will fall on us, do you?" I whispered.

"I hope not," Lou replied.

I watched the beams the rest of the night and listened to the snaps and crackles around us. Neither Lou nor I slept as we waited for daybreak.

The early morning sky was pallid gray, the color of a corpse. I opened the front door and stood there a few moments, taking in the scene. Then I stepped into the front yard and began counting downed trees. Standing in one spot, I counted seventy-five. This did not include the ones behind the house or those deeper in the woods. The carcasses of my prized oak trees lay broken across the ground, their huge root systems ripped out of the bleeding earth, leaving raw, gaping craters in the red clay. Additionally, dogwood trees, pine, hickory, holly, crabapple, redbud, and sycamore were all twisted, toppled, bent, shredded. Over how many generations had those trees stood? I stared dumbfounded at the wounded land. I was overwhelmed. How could we begin to clean up this mess?

The wail of sirens sounded nearby. I looked back at the house, amazed that it still stood. The path of the tornado was visible, dead center through our property, aimed toward our home. I found a small dogwood tree, approximately four feet tall, about fifty feet from the front door. The young tree was still in the ground. Its flexible limbs were twirled around and around its trunk, then tied in a bow knot at the top.

What a strange sight.

The tornado apparently had been on the ground at that point. But it had lifted a little as it passed over the house so that it hit a glancing blow, rather than pulling the structure apart. As I walked back toward the front steps, I considered the fallen oaks that embraced my home with their massive trunks and limbs. A jumble of branches crisscrossed over the face of the house and reached around one side and extended above the roof, effectively creating a shield covering the front of the house. The trees had been pushed over by powerful straight line winds before the arrival of the tornado. Had the trees actually protected the house, providing a buffer between the tornado and the wall of windows across the front?

I began to feel fortunate. My family was unhurt, and my old house was going to get a good facelift. We had recognized its need for remodeling when we bought it, but at the time Lou estimated we would need about five years before we could afford to do so. We had moved in 1985. Now it was 1990. That's five years. I walked back into the house.

"You know, it's Saturday. I'm supposed to work this morning," I told Lou as he came in through the back door. I taught a childbirth class every Saturday morning, but I was going to miss this one.

Lou shook his head. "The cars are blocked. There's no way out of the driveway. My car wasn't totally under the carport, and it's covered up with roofing material."

We began to assess the situation. The roof was heavily damaged, but the house seemed stable. The power was out, and the phone lines were down. A continuous jumble of broken trees covered the road between our house and the highway. This was before the days of cell phones, so we had no way to call out. I looked out a window and studied what remained of the woods that bordered one side of our property. I could see a lot of houses that just yesterday had been hidden by trees. It was Shepherd's old neighborhood, now clearly visible around us.

"The damage doesn't look too bad over there. I'm going to see if I can find someone with a phone line intact."

Lou and I walked back outside and heard the whirl of a helicopter hovering above us. It was from a local television station. I tilted my head upwards.

"Wow, look at that. We're going to be on the news, and wouldn't you know, since we don't have power, we won't even be able to watch ourselves on television."

I headed across the yard toward some houses that seemed undamaged. I had to climb over and through an assortment of fallen trees. I paused and considered the situation when I came to downed power lines. *Uh, this may not be too safe.* Then I very carefully climbed over them too. I finally made my way into the neighboring subdivision. I picked the closest front door and knocked.

"I'm sorry to bother you so early," I said after I introduced myself to the woman who answered the door, "but our place was damaged in the storm last night, and I really need to make some phone calls. Is your phone still working?"

The woman and her husband welcomed me warmly. They introduced themselves as Sara Anne and Jim, and they too were the parents of three boys. Yes, their phone was still working, and they were glad to let me use it. I called my friend Susan, who also taught childbirth classes, and she quickly agreed to teach my class for me. Then I called my parents to let them know we were OK. My parents lived about an hour away. I wasn't sure what the news reports from our area would be, and I didn't want them to worry about us. I didn't realize it, but by calling Susan and my parents, I had started a phone chain that sent our distress signal out to the world.

I talked to Sarah Anne and Jim a few more minutes. They were such nice people. We had a lot in common, and it was a shame that it had taken a tornado to introduce us. Then I said goodbye and started back toward my own house.

I paused again in our front yard and became conscious of a ghostly, unnatural stillness. Normally, a chorus of many voices—chirps, twitters, cackles, and other animal calls—began during the dark blue hour before sunrise, and continued to rise up as the brilliant glow from the sun's upper rim appeared over the horizon, until a crescendo of wild music spilled out of the forest to herald the new day. But now, the atmosphere was silenced, stunned by the blows of the night.

I gazed over the damp, pale sky and searched the remaining trees. Nothing. All the birds and little woodland animals were gone. I tried to imagine what it had been like for the creatures of the forest when those savage winds blasted through without pity, even as my family hunkered down within the protective walls of our house. Later that day I found one dead squirrel, and we saw a couple of living ones that were staggering about in shock, but the remainder of the tree dwellers had been carried away into oblivion. For us, the tornado created a colossal mess and was an enormous inconvenience and expense, but it also presented us with an opportunity to improve both house and gardens. For the surrounding wildlife, the tornado was a catastrophe.

We gave the boys their breakfast and listened to a battery powered radio. We live in a tornado prone area. Over the years some of the most lethal funnels in the nation have hit our region. In 1933, a tornado destroyed most of Helena, and it took many long years for the town to recover. In the scheme of all things, ours was a localized event that damaged property but fortunately took no lives. The storm that brought our tornado was mentioned briefly on the national news, and then the rest of the country moved on to more important events. We also would move on, but for a long time the tornado shadowed us, affecting our lives in numerous ways. Since then, I have seen many disasters of much larger scope and devastation covered by television news channels, and my heart goes out to the people involved in those tragedies. If our tornado impacted us as it did, I can imagine how difficult recovery must be for persons suffering through truly dire circumstances.

The first step for us was to clear the road so that we could get out. With big holes in the roof and with downed power lines across the property, we needed to find a safer place to stay, at least until the house was somewhat habitable. Lou got out the chain saw and went to work clearing trees, starting at the carport behind the house. People showed up to help, including Jim, our newly discovered neighbor on the other side of the woods. My father, age seventy at the time, brought his chain saw to Helena and, starting at the highway, began cutting his way toward us. George, my brother, was trying to get through when a police barricade stopped him.

"Sorry," the policeman said, "outsiders aren't being allowed into this area."

"Look, officer, my sister is in there with three small children. She needs me." He made my situation sound desperate. The policeman looked into the back of my brother's pickup truck at his chain saw and other equipment.

"OK. You can pass."

He waved my brother through, and soon George was helping my dad at the other end of our road. Mike, my oldest brother, coming from another direction, was also able to get in and joined them. Neighbors, friends, and family labored all day to clear the road. Eventually my dad's crew and Lou's group met up in the middle. Piles of broken trees lined the entire road. The roar of chain saws was a sound that would resonate throughout the neighborhood for many months.

Food appeared. Of course. Lots of fried chicken and pizza. As I said, you always get food.

We continued to gauge the damage to our home. The tornado had ripped one of the brick chimneys from the roof and flung it into the parking area out back. Air conditioning duct work lay tangled on top of the house. George had brought some huge blue plastic tarps, and the men worked to fasten these over damaged areas of the roof.

We kept finding metal tubes of assorted lengths in different parts of the yard. We puzzled over this until we realized it was our large wind chime that had hung high in a tree, now torn apart and flung in every direction.

Mark, age four, considered the situation as he watched all the activity. He hadn't said much that day. He finally turned to me. "I don't think I like tornados," he said.

I was worried about our dog.

"Have you seen Shepherd?" I asked my neighbors. They all shook their heads.

"I'm sure he ran from the tornado and found shelter in someone's basement. He's probably just fine." Lou tried to reassure me, as well as himself. I shut my mind to fearful thoughts and concentrated on immediate tasks in front of me. Neither of us could tolerate the idea of Shepherd lying dead or injured under a fallen tree somewhere.

At the end of the day, after the men had cleared the road enough for us to get out, we packed the kids into the minivan and drove to the Residence Inn to spend the night. We returned to the house Sunday morning, and I anxiously looked to see if Shepherd was waiting for us. But he wasn't there, and our concern deepened. He finally showed up Monday afternoon while I was standing outside talking to an insurance agent. He slipped in quietly and sat down beside me, unhurt and acting as if he had just come back from a casual stroll.

The tornado mangled the fence that surrounded the dog yard. Susie roamed from place to place, checking out the damage to her territory.

"Hey, Mom, look at Susie!"

We were outside, and Josh pointed to the woods between our house and the valley. A large, partially uprooted pine tree was leaning over at about a forty-five degree angle to the ground. Susie was at least twenty feet up in the air, carefully balancing herself as she walked up the incline of the tree trunk. All her life she had been wishing she could get into a tree, and now she could do it. Sadly, she found no birds or squirrels.

Chrissie, the sweet, honey-colored cocker spaniel that belonged to our neighbors Ed and Pat, appeared at our doorstep, shivering and seeking solace. Ed and Pat were out of town, and Chrissie had endured the tornado alone, outside on their carport. Chrissie was a homebody who rarely wandered out of her own yard, but today she was needing human comfort.

Chrissie was deeply affected by the tornado. After that day, if there was a storm and nobody was at her house to let her in, she would hurry up to our place. The first time this happened, I found her inside the back entrance to my house, her little muddy paw prints covering the tile floor. Susie and Shepherd lay just outside the open door on the carport. Shepherd had discovered that he could open the back door, unless it was very firmly closed, with a good shove. Apparently he had pushed it so that Chrissie could get inside.

We stayed at the Residence Inn for three weeks. We returned to the house each morning to take care of the animals and to supervise cleanup. At last power and telephone services were restored, and we moved back into our battered house. Blue plastic tarps still covered the roof, and the main bedroom and its bath were unusable. Later, a worker discovered damaged electrical wiring, still live, in the ceiling above our bed. He said that it was a miracle the house had not burned down.

We moved all three boys into one bedroom, with Mark assigned a sleeping bag between his brothers' twin beds. Lou and I put a mattress on the floor in Mark's room, which was water-damaged but livable. The radiant heating system that warmed our wood and tile floors still worked, so we didn't worry about being cold. However, the air conditioning system, which ran through the attic, had been destroyed. We hoped to have a new one in working order by summer.

Just one month after the tornado, we did what everybody should do following a disaster—we went to Disney World! Lou had won this trip in a sales contest, all expenses paid, airplane tickets already purchased. It was our first non-summertime vacation. We thought a March vacation would avoid some of the heat and crowds of a more traditional summer vacation to Florida. We wanted to go. We needed to go. We put Susie and Shepherd in a boarding kennel with assurances that they would be together. Then we shut the door behind us and went. The wreck would be waiting for us when we returned.

We took lots of pictures and saved up memories during our week away from reality. We rode the rides and watched fireworks. We ate too much delicious food. The boys enjoyed meeting all the Disney characters, though one morning when we were eating at a restaurant Josh got more than he expected. Goofy the Dog came in and approached our table. He bowed to Josh, and Josh stood up to shake his hand. But Goofy began tickling Josh instead, and before it was over, Josh was screeching and rolling on the floor. Everyone in the building was laughing, most of all Josh.

Later that day we saw a robot standing by itself on a small plaza. The metal creature was about three feet tall, and it resembled an astronaut with a silver suit and gold helmet. It was attached to a bright red scooter. To our surprise, the robot said hello to us, in a distinctive metallic voice.

"Hello, who are you?" Mark replied.

The robot gave us its technical name, which involved some letters and numbers, then asked Mark, "What is your name?"

"My name is Mark."

"Hello, Mark. It is good to meet you. Where are you from?"

"I'm from Helena, Alabama."

"Helena? This is where there was some bad weather?"

Our mouths fell open. Was this a trick, or were we seeing an amazing form of artificial intelligence? Whichever it was, Mark was having a great conversation. As he continued to chat with the robot, a crowd began to gather around us. Soon people were taking photos, marveling over my four-year-old son and the robot as the two carried on a dialogue about robotics—a conversation that was far above my comprehension but that Mark seemed to understand perfectly.

After a while, the robot said, "I must go now. I must go charge my batteries. Goodbye, Mark. I enjoyed talking with you." We all waved as the robot drove away on its scooter.

That was the day I realized my youngest son was going to become an engineer. This was confirmed about a year later when Mark announced he wanted a lemonade stand. He never sold a single glass of lemonade, but the detailed plans he drew for the lemonade stand hung on our refrigerator for over a year. We still have the drawing.

Another highlight of our trip to Disney World was Discovery Island with its giant tortoises and exotic talking birds. While we were there, one of the birds heard me hollering for Sam, and a moment later the bird began mimicking me.

"Sa-am! Sa-am!" It must have liked the sound of the name, because we could hear the bird squawking my son's name for the rest of the morning, up until we departed. Many of these birds live for fifty years or more—some macaws have lived up to 100 years! So for all I know, that bird may even yet be calling for Sam.

Toward the end of the week, we heard news reports about heavy storms in Alabama. We ignored the reports and concentrated on squeezing every bit of fun we could get out of this vacation.

Coming home, heavy wind and rain buffeted the airplane as we flew into the Birmingham airport late at night, and we cringed when we heard something about ten inches of rain in two days. We were dead-tired as we drove back to Helena in the dark. I watched our Ford Aerostar's windshield wipers working steadily against the downpour. Sheets of water were streaming across the car windows when we pulled into our driveway around midnight. The boys were sleeping in the back of the car. Neither Lou nor I had commented much about the rain or the plastic sheeting that covered the roof.

"Stay here," Lou said as he stopped next to the carport. "I'm going to check things out." He and I were thinking the same thing.

He got out of the minivan and sloshed toward the house. I sat in the dark, gazing at the waterfall cascading over the windshield, and waited for him to return. He came out of the house a few minutes later.

"Well, how bad is it?" I asked.

"It's bad."

Vacation was over. Water at least a half-inch deep covered most of the floors. We put the children to bed and began placing buckets, pots, and pans in strategic places under leaks. We mopped for hours. We used all the blankets and towels in the house to soak up water, then lugged the heavy things to the bathtub, where we laboriously squeezed the water out before reusing them.

The next morning I noticed a huge sag that was growing ominously in the wallpapered ceiling of the living room.

"Lou, come here quick! We need to move the furniture! Now!"

We rushed to shove couches and tables out from under the menacing bulge. Within moments, as the seams of the wallpaper ruptured and a great hole in the ceiling appeared, pent-up water gushed down into the room. It was filthy brown and smelled like sewage.

Some of it had been trapped since the tornado, ripening in the space above the living room for over a month. The overpowering stench of the putrid water spread through the house. Disney World was long ago and far away as we cleaned up one more nasty, sopping mess.

Emotions can be surprising. I didn't cry. I didn't feel depressed. There was too much to do. We were trying to maintain a semblance of normalcy amidst the chaos. The boys went to school, I taught childbirth classes, and Lou's medical sales job kept him as busy as usual. Lou did as much as he could, but because he was frequently on the road, many of the responsibilities of putting the house back together fell to me. I had to find somebody to draw up plans for the remodeling of the house. I had to talk to insurance agents, and I had to talk to the bank about financing. I had to fill out forms and make phone calls. I had to find a contractor. For a long time I plodded onward, accomplishing one task at a time, making one decision, then another, seemingly numb to it all.

Then one day a man came to cut down an oak tree that was leaning dangerously toward the house. Rather than using ropes to carefully direct the fall of the tree, he thoughtlessly dropped the trunk of the tree through the middle of three of my forty-year-old boxwoods, splitting them to pieces.

"Oh, they'll sprout right back," he said.

He didn't know what he was talking about. Real boxwoods—not their cheaper imitations—grow slowly. I treasured my boxwoods. These iconic plants are often featured in antique gardens of the South. I had been thankful that mine had come through the tornado undamaged.

After the man left, I calmly got into the minivan, shut the door, and then wailed as if he had slaughtered my children.

Sounds of hammering and sawing echoed daily around us as other houses were put back in order, but the months passed and our damaged house still sat under its blue plastic tarps. Everything took much longer than we had anticipated because we had decided to do some major remodeling, enlarging the main bedroom and raising the roof to accommodate several new upstairs rooms. We had to wait weeks for drawings after the designer's secretary had a heart attack. (Apparently the guy couldn't work without this particular secretary!) The bank wouldn't give us any money without the drawings, and we couldn't start building without the bank's approval.

Work on the house finally began in June, four months after the tornado. Tom, the contractor, was a nice man who listened to my ideas. He was honest and dependable. He didn't smoke, curse, or consume alcohol in front of our children. But we soon discovered that he was exceptionally slow, a man who liked to talk and who worked at a tedious pace. We would go through the entire summer without air conditioning.

It was a hot, hot, hot summer. Without the protective cover of the trees, the full force of the brutal sun beat down over the house. Before church on Sundays, I would get into the car immediately prior to leaving and then, after turning on the vehicle's air conditioning, I would squint at the small mirror located in the middle of the sun visor and apply my make-up. If I put it on in the house, it would be dripping off my face by the time I got out the door. We ordered new windows for the entire house: double insulated, argon filled, Low-E glass. Very nice.

We celebrated in late autumn when the heating and cooling specialists at last turned on the new air conditioning system. The very next morning we woke to the first frost of the season.

One day that summer I surveyed our shattered realm as Lou and I raked debris from the front lawn. The familiar sound of a chain saw came from a neighboring yard, and smoke rose from great piles of brush that were burning along our road. Craters left behind by uprooted trees still pockmarked the land.

"This is terrible," I said to Lou. "This place looks like it's been bombed."

I sighed over the sad state of my yard. Azaleas were shriveling under the sun. Hostas were drying up and disappearing. The center of our property needed to be completely replanted with new trees and sun loving plants, and my budget for landscaping was zero. The house had to come first.

We continued to clean up pieces of broken limbs. A few fat clouds appeared in the sky, and a breeze began to blow. Lou stopped and stood leaning against his rake. He looked worried.

"Sure is a lot of wind out here," he commented.

Inwardly, I felt it too. It was absurd, but for years after the tornado even a cooling puff of air caused a heightening of the senses and a little twist of the gut.

A splotch of yellow color caught my attention. When I investigated, I had to smile.

"Look what I found," I called.

It was a sunflower, and its cheerful face encouraged me. I had never planted sunflowers, and I guessed that a bird had dropped a seed there. It was a single bloom in the middle of my torn-up yard, but I felt like the sunflower was a promise: *Hang in there, things are going to get better.* I looked around at the trees within the sections of our property that were less damaged by the tornado. The birds and squirrels and other little critters were coming back. I bought a pack of zinnia seeds and planted them.

That fall my friend Nancy gave me some small saplings that she dug from her yard—a redbud, some dogwoods, and a mock orange. I searched local nurseries for bargain plants, and I found some inexpensive seedling Japanese maple trees.

I have a real fondness for Japanese maples. Soon after we married, Lou and I had purchased a small one, and for years it grew in a big pot. When we moved to Helena, I planted it out in the front yard under the oak trees, where it thrived. I called it our marriage tree. During the storm, massive tree trunks came down all around this special tree, but not a single limb of our marriage tree was broken. It was the only tree in the center of our property that came through the tornado untouched.

I planted my new seedlings and dreamed of what they would look like in a decade. There is a saying in landscaping that you must either have lots of money or lots of patience, and the less you have of one, the more you need of the other. How true.

Almost everything I put in my yard was tiny. I looked out the window one day and was horrified to see a worker standing with his boot atop one of my new Japanese maple seedlings. I rushed out to fuss at him.

"You are standing on my tree!"

Puzzled, the man looked down at the twig trapped below his boot. "This is a tree?"

For several years I had to mark each plant with a ring of rocks so that Lou would not mistake it for a weed. I would take him out into the yard and point to a baby stick poking out of the ground, telling him to be careful not to step on it or to cut it down.

Not everything I planted lived, but some of it did, in spite of children on bicycles and digging dogs and hungry bugs and strange fungal things that appeared overnight. These are tough plants that have survived months of drought and days of torrential rains—strong, Deep South plants that can also take an occasional blast of frozen air from the North. People often admire these survivors, and (not knowing about all the dead ones) they sometimes comment on my remarkable green thumb.

These days, visitors who drive up our road are welcomed into a lush setting of mature trees and many flowering shrubs. The seasons feature plants with beautiful blooms and colorful foliage. Fragrant star jasmine, a flowering vine, covers a cast-iron arch at the entry to the patio, and coral honeysuckle grows on a picket fence that marks the entry into an area for fruits and vegetables. There is an herb bed, blueberries and blackberries, apple trees, a persimmon tree, a fig tree, and a plot for miscellaneous vegetables. I walk through our property along meandering trails lined with perennials and flowering shrubs. A curving stone stairway leads to a peaceful woodland garden with cushy moss paths that wind through the trees. The woodland garden features a fern glade, as well as many native azaleas and other shade-loving plants. All the pass-along trees from my friend Nancy are fully grown now, and their pink and white blossoms are a reminder of the enduring value of friendship. The tiny Japanese maple seedlings have grown into trees of character with undulating limbs and leaves that shimmer when backlit by the sun. Our marriage tree is about twenty-five feet tall now and just as wide.

The remodeled house sits pretty with its energy efficient windows and expanded dimensions, and through the changing seasons I enjoy my spot by the large living room windows. I watch a multitude of birds, chipmunks and squirrels, rabbits, bees and butterflies, and other little critters that inhabit our property. Sometimes it seems almost a dream that this place belongs to us. My dad, admiring the property, once said that the tornado was one of the best things that ever happened. Maybe so.

CHAPTER EIGHT

WHISKERS

"Oh, Sam. He's so tiny. Where did you find him?"

Sam was carefully holding together his cupped palms as he lifted them up for me to see. An infant gray squirrel was curled in his hands, its body barely covered with thin fur and its eyes still sealed shut.

"I found him on the ground beside a big pine tree. I didn't see his mother anywhere."

"He must have fallen out of his nest during the storm," I said, remembering the previous night's high winds. I had a sinking feeling as I regarded my son. He trusted his mother to save this baby squirrel, which was probably going to die no matter what I did.

Still, it was possible. My parents had rescued a baby squirrel when I was in college. They named him Dale. One weekend I went home for a visit, and when I entered their glassed-in front porch, Dale introduced himself to me by running up the inside of my pants leg. He got stuck about midway between knee and crotch. Dale and I both screeched. I had to take off my jeans, right there on the front porch, to get him out. Soon afterwards, my dad built a wooden squirrel house and placed it in a tree in the back yard. Dale liked his new living arrangements and lived there for several years, choosing a mate and raising several sets of babies inside the structure. The squirrel often sat on my dad's shoulder when he went outside to visit Dale, and passersby would slow down to gawk.

"We'll see what we can do," I told Sam. "Go get some old towels and a box to put him in. I think we have an eye dropper I can use to feed him."

As I hunted for the eye dropper and then prepared a warm concoction of milk and corn syrup, I grumbled to myself. It was just over twelve months since the tornado, and it had been a rough year. I didn't want any new responsibilities or new pets.

However, the poor thing would be dead soon, and it wouldn't hurt to make it comfortable. I held the animal in my hand and placed the tip of the eye dropper in its tiny mouth. To my surprise, he began to suck eagerly, emptying one full eyedropper, then another. Sam, confident that he had delivered his squirrel into competent hands, departed for new adventures. I began to feed the animal every couple hours, and soon he was clasping the eyedropper with his front paws, holding it just like a baby with a bottle. He was so cute. Maybe he would survive after all.

Before I went to bed that night, I faced a dilemma. How often do baby squirrels feed during the night? Should I get up in the wee hours of the morning to feed him? I wasn't willing to get up as often as every two hours, but I did decide to set the alarm for one night feeding. Two o'clock should be about right. The next morning I was a bit sleepy, but the baby squirrel seemed to be doing just fine as he curled contentedly amidst a soft wrapping of towels.

I continued to regularly feed him, and a few days later he was finishing a meal when his eyes opened for the first time. I looked in wonder into the eyes of this little creature in my hands, and he stared right back at me, absorbing his first view of the world. I knew at that moment, as he fixed his beastie little gaze upon my face, that bonds were forming for both of us.

I was his comfort-giver, his protector, his source of nourishment. He already was familiar with my touch, my smell, and the sounds that I made. Now he knew what I looked like. He trusted me completely. For better or for worse, I had become a squirrel mama. The animal soon became comfortable with all members of his new family, and I suspected that he thought he, too, was human.

I knew nothing about being mama to a squirrel. It was a fearful responsibility. I hoped that I wouldn't irreparably interfere with his ability to live a normal life. I hoped instinct would take over for such things as communicating with other squirrels, mating, building nests, and keeping himself safe from predators. I wasn't sure. I read everything the *World Book Encyclopedia* had to say about squirrels. While there was good information about the appearance of different types of squirrels, their sizes, colors, and periods of gestation, I didn't learn anything about mothering one. There was no internet in those days, with easy access to information on almost every imaginable topic. I was on my own.

Andrew, a young friend who was visiting one day, observed our squirrel as the young critter played with my boys.

"You ought to call him Whiskers," Andrew said, "because he has such long whiskers."

It was true. The squirrel sat up in Sam's palm, looking around and appearing quite intelligent and inquisitive about life. He had black eyes and long whiskers like a cat's.

Within weeks Whiskers was eating tiny pieces of fruits and vegetables, chopped nuts, and store-bought hamster food. He grew rapidly. Soon he had a nice bushy tail and was covered with a good coat of gray fur.

Before the tornado, there had been a breezeway between the house and Lou's office, but when we remodeled the house, we had enclosed it to create a new back entry hall. This spacious area, along with the laundry room and Lou's office, became squirrel world. A stairway led to several new upstairs rooms, not yet finished. A door at one end of the hallway opened to the carport. On the opposite end of the hallway was the door to the outside area that had previously been our fenced-in dog yard, although we had yet to replace the fence destroyed by the tornado. Lou's office door was next to the stairway, and across from here was the door leading to the laundry room and the main part of the house. The hallway contained an old bench that had sat on Lou's parents' front porch during his childhood, and there was also a child's tractor hitched to a wagon full of work boots. A pegboard covered most of the wall next to the laundry room door, and it conveniently held assorted gardening tools and supplies. The pegboard was a good place for Whiskers to practice his climbing skills. He liked to scamper up and down and around the hedge clippers, pruning saws, rakes, and hoes. Sometimes he would climb into one of the boots in the wagon, then poke his head out and chatter at me as I walked past.

Whiskers loved my husband. Lou would be sitting at his desk, doing paper work or talking on the telephone with an important client, when Whiskers would dart into his office and scurry up the outside of his pants leg. He would settle into Lou's lap, demanding attention, wanting his ears scratched and then rolling over for a tummy rub. Once satisfied, he would curl up and soon would be sleeping in his daddy's lap while Lou continued his phone calls and other office work. Whiskers was as affectionate as any puppy, and he liked to play. Every night he returned to a towel lined wire cage. I would click my tongue and call his name, and he would hurry to me, ready for bedtime.

It may have seemed that Whiskers would make a fine pet, but squirrels are wild creatures with unruly natural instincts, and they grow up to have sharp claws and teeth. They were never meant to be kept captive inside a house. I realized my guardianship had to be temporary. I did not take Whiskers outside of the house during the first month after he came to us. But as I watched him, I knew I needed to introduce him to his natural habitat.

My heart was heavy with concern. What would happen to little Whiskers when we went outside?

The time came one morning in late spring. We had built the boys a new playground in a cleared area between the house and the valley. The playground equipment included an L-shaped swing set with a selection of swings. The short section of the L held a tire swing that was a favorite with both children and adults. The play area also contained a tall climbing tower with two levels. The lower level was about five feet off the ground and had a tubular slide coming down from it. The upper level was twice as high and had a much longer aluminum slide for a fast and thrilling exit to the ground. There was a climbing net, sliding pole, and an assortment of ladders that provided access to the different levels. The various components of the massive wooden play set came in a do-it-yourself kit that had arrived on a truck the size of a large moving van. It took a team of muscular relatives a couple of weekends to put it all together. When we built it, Lou had joked that we could train marines on it, so I decided it would be adequate for a squirrel.

I cradled Whiskers in my arm as I climbed to the top level of the tower. I sat down and settled him into my lap. It was a perfect day. I breathed in the refreshing air and tilted my head upwards. A few puffy white clouds drifted across the pale blue sky, and a breeze whispered amidst the leaves in the dogwood and oak trees around us. Mockingbirds were singing, and I could hear the squeaking of squirrels nearby.

"This is your home, Whiskers. Those squirrels may be your relatives. What do you think?"

Whiskers crept to the edge of the tower and peered over the precipice. He immediately gave a shriek of alarm and jumped back into my lap.

Oh, no! He was ruined. Imagine a squirrel that was afraid of heights!

I could feel his tiny heart racing as he huddled in my lap. "It's OK. Don't be afraid." I stroked his fur and tried to reassure him.

Eventually his curiosity overcame his fear, and he began to explore the top of the tower, flapping his tail with excitement when he once again gazed over the edge. We stayed up there about thirty minutes, listening to the sounds of the woodland and enjoying the crisp air and the greenery that surrounded us.

I took Whiskers out to the playground every day for the next week, and before long he was comfortable playing on the tower. He explored both levels of the structure, and he also enjoyed climbing up and across the big wooden beams of the swing set. He made no attempt to run away.

When playtime was over, I would click my tongue and call to him, "Come, Whiskers." He would hurry down from his perch atop the play equipment, then scamper beside my feet as I headed back toward the house. He was an obedient squirrel. I wished all my children would come so promptly when called.

The next step was to let Whiskers climb a tree. My heart was heavy as I thought about it—once he got into a tree, he probably would take off, and I would never see him again.

Yet I had to do it, because squirrels are born to be free. So one morning I took him out behind the house and placed him at the base of a pine tree that was about thirty feet tall. He clung to the tree trunk and looked at me.

"Go on, " I said, encouraging him by pointing up into the tree. "You can do it."

Whiskers eyed the tree, then eyed me. He slowly began to climb, gripping the rough brown pine bark. Like a free-solo climber, he cautiously pulled himself upward one leg at a time, feeling his way, and then when he reached about ten feet, he stopped and stared down at me. He flapped his tail several times, then crept up a few more feet. Suddenly, he turned and raced back down to the base of the tree. Looking at me, he squeaked loudly. Then he scurried back up the tree, faster and higher this time. He paused a moment, then came back down the trunk just far enough so that he could see me eye to eye. He began jabbering at me. I don't speak squirrel talk, but I could understand every word.

Look, Ma! Look at me, see what I can do! Watch me!

Back up the trunk he darted, confidently accelerating up, up until he reached the very top branch of the pine tree. From this lofty perch he called out to all creation, exulting in his prowess and proclaiming himself King of the World. I was very proud of my squirrel.

I once read an article by an "expert" who asserted that animals don't have emotions similar to humans. The person also assumed that the size of an animal's brain determines its intelligence, so a creature such as a squirrel would have extremely limited intellect. This opinion was based on unfounded preconceptions rather than research. Notions that animals lack minds and are incapable of reasoning were handed down from the seventeenth century and have been thoroughly debunked by modern studies. Animals are much more complex and demonstrate much more intelligence than we imagined. We must remember that animals are not humans, and we cannot expect them to think or to behave like humans. We may test animals according to human standards, and this will only prove that some animals are more like humans than others. In fact, an animal's aptitudes often are in areas beyond human comprehension. No doubt, if I were being judged according to squirrel standards, I would fail miserably.

Whiskers was a rodent, but he showed affection, joy, pride, and fear. He attempted to communicate with me. He responded to his name. And in the end, despite his abnormal beginnings, he knew he was a squirrel and not a human.

After Whiskers had been exploring the pine tree for a while, I called out to him, clicking my tongue.

"Whiskers! Come, Whiskers!" Like an obedient dog, he hurried to me. Down the tree he came, and I gratefully gathered him into my arms and returned to the house.

Whiskers and I developed a daily routine. I let him out every morning, and he spent his day in nearby trees, exploring and discovering the abundant food sources in our woods. About noon I checked up on him. I stood on the gravel parking area behind the house and called him. Out of the woods he hurried, as if he had been waiting for our midday visit. I offered some verbal encouragement and an ear scratch before he returned to his exploration and play. Then at the end of each day, he returned to the house, where he spent the night safely inside his wire cage.

One momentous day when I went out for our midday visit, Whiskers did not respond. I walked around the parking area, searching and calling to him. I finally found him in an oak tree on the edge of the gravel parking area, occupied with refurbishing an old squirrel nest. When I called to him again, he looked down at me and chattered back at me from the tree, but he didn't come.

Oh, hi, Mom. I didn't hear you at first. I'm sorry. I'm a little busy. I can't come right now. He continued to stuff leaves into the nest.

I went back into the house and told Lou what Whiskers was doing. "I think it's time for him to stay out at night. He's ready to be on his own."

That evening I did not bring him into the house.

"You can stay out," I told him when he came to me at the end of the day. "You go on back to your nest." I pointed toward the woods.

I watched with heavy heart as he hurried across the parking area and disappeared into the forest. This was it. Graduation day.

In the middle of the night I startled awake when a clap of thunder shook the house. The wind was howling, and rain was pelting against the windows.

"Lou! Are you awake?" I whispered urgently.

"Uh-huh."

"It's storming outside!"

"Uh-huh."

"Whiskers is out there!"

"Uh-huh."

"You think he'll be OK?"

"Uh-huh."

Troubled, I lay unsleeping, as if I had a teenager out late who was driving around town in the thunderstorm. As the storm eased away, I finally drifted back to sleep.

When I woke up the next morning, I jumped out of bed and rushed outside.

"Whiskers! Whiskers!" I clicked my tongue and called him. "Come, Whiskers!"

Soon I heard a familiar jabber coming from a tree. I looked up, and I saw Whiskers sitting on a branch, flapping his tail and telling me all about his night out.

"Come here, Whiskers," I called again.

He came down from the tree and slowly approached me. I could tell he was reluctant to come, but he was doing so because, after all, I was his mama.

Really, Mom, you shouldn't have worried. I can take care of myself now.

He was a fine, healthy, handsome squirrel, with bright eyes and thick fur. He would be a big adult squirrel soon.

I sighed. He would do well. Before long, he would forget about me, and he would find a mate and have a family of his own. My duty was done.

"Goodbye," I called as he turned and jumped onto a nearby tree trunk. I watched as he ran up and then disappeared amidst the leaves.

I never called Whiskers to me again, but sometimes I thought I saw him in the trees. There were a lot of squirrels, and, truthfully, after a while I couldn't tell him from the others. But for years, occasionally I would look out the kitchen window and see a squirrel sitting atop the picnic table on the patio, his eyes fixed on the house. I would smile and wave.

The squirrel would gaze back at me, flap his tail, then hop off the table and hurry back into the trees, where he belonged.

CHAPTER NINE

CAT IN A TREE

Lou and I never had a cat while the boys were growing up. That's a little sad, because I like cats, and I think our boys also would have enjoyed them. There were many animals around our house when I was growing up, as both of my parents loved animals and would freely welcome any sad creature that needed a home. At one time we had seven dogs, ten cats, and a crow! Our cats and dogs were always tolerant, if not completely friendly, toward one another. Among our animals were a mother cat named Susan and a big German shepherd mix named Bruno.

I owe my life to Bruno. He was born on my first birthday, so my parents had a special love for him. He normally wasn't allowed inside the house, because he was big and clumsy and was a real hazard to lamps. However, the Christmas after I had turned two, they made an exception and let him inside while we were decorating the tree. It was a tall Scotch pine, and my dad had sprayed it with flocking before he brought it into the house so that it looked like it was covered with snow. My parents were helping my older brothers to hang popcorn garlands and homemade ornaments on the tree, while I was playing about on the other side of the room, admiring the glittery mess littered across the floor.

Bruno was nearby, and he is the one who saw me pick up a piece of cut wire and poke it into an electrical outlet. A charge of electricity immediately surged through my hand, and the deadly electrical current held me stuck fast to the wire. My mother screamed when she recognized the dangerous situation. But before either of my parents could move toward me, Bruno hurled his body against me and forcefully dislodged me from the electricity. This all happened in an instant, and, except for a burned hand, I was fine.

Bruno also saved one of our cats, a sleek black animal we named Sambo. Susan, the mother cat, once delivered a litter under the house, and after the birth she brought the kittens out, one by one, and placed each of them in the new bed my dad had prepared for her inside a box on the porch. She had settled in with her babies snuggled against her side when Bruno began barking at my dad. The dog headed for the crawlspace under the house, then turned back and barked again. Clearly, he wanted my dad to follow him. Dad lay on his belly and slid under the house to where Bruno guided him. He couldn't see anything at first, but as he pulled to where Bruno was sniffing the ground, he heard a small cry. There was one more tiny kitten. He was solid black, and Susan had overlooked him in the inky darkness of the crawlspace.

The little black kitten that Bruno rescued grew up to be a big, tough tomcat who fought many battles. Sambo had tattered ears, and old scars on his forehead looked like railroad tracks running through the furry landscape. He was a good watchdog(cat). If a strange dog wandered into our yard, he chased it away. If the dog did not get the message soon enough, Sambo would, like a cowboy on a bucking bronco, jump on the dog's back, dig his claws in, and ride the animal out of the yard. A strange dog that met Sambo rarely returned. But Sambo was affectionate toward humans, and he and Bruno were always best buddies.

When Sambo was about ten years old, he brought home a kitten, holding her in his mouth by the scruff of her neck. She was very young—we estimated around six weeks. We never knew where he found her. The kitten had thick, long fur, and we watched in amazement as our battle-hardened tomcat bathed the small creature. It wasn't easy for him. He held the kitten between his front paws and began to lick her, but the kitten's abundant hair kept sticking to his tongue. He would move his head up and down and side to side, working to dislodge the clump of fur from his mouth before trying another patch.

Two weeks later a car ran over Sambo, killing him instantly. Heartbroken, Dad wrapped our beloved cat in a towel and carried him to the back yard for burial. He allowed only Bruno to stand by his side as he laid Sambo to rest. Dad said it was appropriate that the two of them were together at the end of Sambo's life, as they had been at the beginning.

We adopted the orphan kitten, for we were certain that is what Sambo had intended for us to do. She was a beautiful cat with luxurious tortoise-shell fur, mottled gray, orange, and brown. Several gray and white horizontal stripes were above each of her four white paws, like socks sticking out of boots, so we named her Boots.

Our cats were easier to take care of and far cleaner than the dogs. They were fun to play with, and there was something soothing about having a purring cat curled up in one's lap.

Growing up, Lou, unlike me, was never around cats. His sister had a dog, and Lou took care of an assortment of fish inside the ten-gallon tank in his bedroom. But the family possessed an abiding prejudice against cats that had been passed down through the generations from Lou's paternal grandmother. Grandma was a good Christian lady, but she hated cats and had educated her family about the haughty, bloodthirsty nature that was born into the vile creatures.

I can understand Grandma's bias against cats, for her opinion was based upon bad experience. The story I heard was that she lived next door to a woman who owned twenty-six cats. I'm not sure if that is an accurate number or if it has been inflated by legend. Only a few feet separated the houses, and her neighbor's cats subjected poor Grandma to all sorts of indignities. They yowled under her bedroom window at night and hissed at her when she went out to get the morning paper. They stank up the yard. They fought with one another. They slept on top of her car and left paw prints all over it. And worst of all, they killed birds and left fragments of decomposing corpses scattered across her lawn. So Grandma had a right to her opinion, though I believe her argument should have been with the thoughtless, irresponsible neighbor rather than with the cats themselves.

It doesn't have to be that way. One has to understand a cat. The personality traits of cats are similar to those of humans. If one treats a cat with respect and allows for its individual characteristics, one can develop a genuine bond with the cat. Yes, a cat is a predator. So are humans. A cat can enrich a person's life, and I felt certain that if Lou got to know one, he would agree with me. A positive personal relationship is the easiest path to understanding and will surely break the power of any prejudice founded in ignorance. But Lou's bias against cats was developed during the impressionable years of his childhood. He thought he already knew everything he needed to know about cats, and that was the end of the discussion. It is hard to fight that kind of prejudice.

But it can be done.

In the beginning, I was unaware of Lou's intolerance of cats. I met my future husband one morning after I had worked a hard night on a post-op cardiac surgery floor. I was talking to a coworker as we waited for an elevator, and I started to follow her when the elevator door slid open. Then I stopped and looked toward the cafeteria, at the end of a long corridor painted what I fondly called "puke pink." I wondered if I could make myself stay awake a little longer. I wanted to get home to bed as soon as possible, but the gnawing sensation in my stomach couldn't be ignored.

"You go on," I told my coworker. "I'm going to get something to eat first. I haven't had a bite since yesterday afternoon, and I don't have the energy to make breakfast."

I walked toward the cafeteria, not thinking at all about the possibilities any new day may bring. I had some suspicious yellow stain on my white uniform, my makeup had disappeared hours ago, and tendrils of hair had escaped from my long ponytail and hung wild around my face. I was too tired to care. I felt like a soggy towel on a storm-battered clothesline.

I joined a stream of hospital employees and visitors that converged upon steaming metal containers of bacon, sausage, scrambled eggs, grits, biscuits, and gravy, then moved on toward the coffee maker and the fruit and juice bar. There was plenty of heavy food for hungry folks and comfort food for those who needed comforting. I looked for Mrs. Montgomery, the cafeteria worker who piled huge portions onto plates with a smile and promises of "nothing but the very best." Her shining black eyes and jovial spirit ministered to all those souls who passed her way, and her medicine was always more palatable than that offered in other parts of the hospital.

I didn't see her, and I sighed. My senses were on the edge of numbness. If this line didn't start moving faster, I was going to fall asleep, right there on my feet. The clatter of dishes and jumble of conversation did little to rouse me. My eyelids drooped as the sounds of the cafeteria began to recede. Maybe breakfast wasn't such a good idea, after all. I yawned and reached for some grapefruit juice.

A clear voice behind me said, "Now, you can't be as tired and sleepy as I am."

Surprised, I jerked my eyelids open and looked over my shoulder. A tall, thin guy with a bush of curly brown hair and wire rim glasses was smiling at me. He wore a white jacket over a gray scrub suit. He had a great smile.

My senses prickled to consciousness.

"Really? Where have you been working?" Beginning to feel much perkier, I batted my eyelashes at him. This man was cute.

"Emergency room, and I'm pulling a double. When I leave here, I'm headed for the cath lab for another shift."

There was that smile again, wide and genuine, and twinkling blue eyes with little crinkles at the corners. The name *Louis Elliott* was stitched onto his coat, and he told me to call him Lou. I learned that he was working as a radiological technologist while he took classes at

UAB. After paying for our meals, we sat down at a table to continue our conversation.

At that moment, I looked at him and knew he was my future husband. (Lou has no recollection of having similar thoughts about me.) We talked on for nearly an hour about our respective jobs, about our mutual admiration of Mrs. Montgomery, and about our backgrounds and education. When it was time for him to go to the cath lab, where he would spend the day helping with heart catheterizations, Lou pulled a pen and a palm-sized black book out of his coat pocket.

"Can I have your phone number?" he asked.

You're kidding. I hesitated a moment while I considered this charmer and his little black book, then answered, "I don't know you very well, but my number is…"

I carried an unexpected rush of happiness home. It was like enduring the storms of the night, then looking up in the morning to behold a gift come floating down from the clouds. I told my roommate that I had met a VIP, a very important person. I sometimes wonder what would have happened if I hadn't been in the cafeteria line that morning.

We married two years later, and two years after that I found his little black book stashed away in a drawer. I pulled the book out and held it in my hand, pondering.

Why is this thing still around? Well, hmmm, can it hurt to look?

I flipped through its pages, puzzled at first, then realized I was looking at, not a list of romantic partners, but car maintenance records. I laughed. My phone number was the only one in there.

During the first year after we married, we lived in a small red brick apartment building across the street from Avondale Park in

Birmingham. The neighborhood was a bit sketchy. The buildings on our street were a mixture of moderately dilapidated older homes, modest apartments, and a couple of gas stations. A church on the corner sounded its bell on Sunday mornings, calling the brethren of the neighborhood to worship, although I'm not sure how many responded.

During the first half of the twentieth century, Avondale Park had been a popular destination with spring-fed wading pools, a large pavilion, paved walkways, benches and picnic tables. At one time it featured a zoo. But as the surrounding area aged and began to decline, the park had lost much of its attraction. However, it was decently maintained and nice enough if we avoided it during the risky hours when the drug dealers were out. We liked to go over there to feed the ducks and geese, though I learned to be careful around them. One summer day when I was wearing shorts, I bent over to throw crumbs to the ducks in the pond, and an aggressive goose came from behind, stuck his beak up inside the leg of my shorts, and nipped me on the bottom.

School and jobs at the university occupied most of our time. The apartment was our place to pause, to eat, and to sleep. Our tiny apartment accommodated a six-foot couch that stretched from one end of the living room to the other, with only a few feet left over to move around. Almost all the living in the space had to be done on the couch. It wasn't a real couch—it was an old army cot, dredged up from a relative's basement. One leg was broken, and we propped that side up with bricks. Not pretty, but it served the purpose, and with a few toss pillows it wasn't too bad.

We had no television. We had little time to watch it, and we rarely missed it. It was easy to keep up with soap operas by occasionally catching a few minutes of programming in the staff lounge at work. In fact, we didn't own a TV until my mother gave us one when Sam and Josh were preschoolers. She worried that her grandchildren might not grow up to be completely normal if they never saw *Sesame Street*.

The kitchen was the largest room in our apartment. It held a small dinette set with a square table and two chairs, which I had purchased second-hand from the unit secretary at work. Our bedroom was filled up by a queen-size bed and a dresser. Another bedroom was the size of a moderate walk-in closet, and this was Lou's office.

Traffic whizzed by a few feet from our living room window. A wide slab of asphalt in front of the apartment building was used for parking. There was no lawn except for some crab grass and other assorted weeds that sprouted beside the sidewalk.

One dreary winter evening we were in the living room when we heard a woeful cry outside our door. I was sitting on the army cot, reading a book, and I looked up as Lou went to investigate. He opened the front door and beheld a gray kitten huddled on the walkway in front of him, shivering from the freezing rain.

By now I knew that Lou hated cats, at least in theory, just as his father and his father's mother before him had hated cats. In theory is one thing. Having a sad little animal, cold and hungry, sitting at his feet, begging for help—well, that transcends theory. Lou picked up the kitty and brought it into the apartment.

I raised my eyebrows but didn't say much. Lou carried the animal toward the kitchen.

"Do you think it'll drink some warm milk?"

"Oh, I think so," I answered. Behind my book I was smiling.

I heard the refrigerator door open and pans rattling. After a while Lou called out from the kitchen.

143

"This cat is sick!"

"Oh, no! What's wrong?" I put down the book and hurried into the kitchen.

"I think it has pneumonia. Listen to that noise coming out of its chest. It has rales."

Rales is a medical term that refers to the rattling or crackling noise that lungs make when they are congested. Sure enough, from across the room I could hear a loud rumbling sound coming from the little cat, a resonance that signaled, not pneumonia, but a peaceful spirit and a warm body and a full belly. The kitten was purring.

Lou, whose only physical contact with a cat had been with a feline cadaver in the biology lab, had never heard a cat purr. I laughed and poked fun at my husband. But I wished I hadn't, for soon he put the kitty back outside. After all, our tiny urban apartment was no place for a cat, and we were far too busy to keep it.

The next morning we found the kitten dead in the street in front of the apartment. We both were shocked. In my heart I felt the heavy, remorseful pain of guilt. Lou's look told me that he felt the same, and I caught a glimpse of something that told me, given the right situation, Lou could care for a cat.

Through the years the right situation was elusive. Susie, the hunting dog, liked to chase cats, and any cat who dared to come onto our property was in jeopardy. Nevertheless, I was tempted one December day a few weeks before Mark was born, when a fluffy gray kitten appeared on our doorstep. Sam and Josh wanted to keep it. Lou was noncommittal, which was a much more positive response than I expected. That meant the decision was mine. But the timing was all wrong. Soon I would have a newborn to care for, and we already had Susie and Shepherd. I decided to put a flyer up on the giant bulletin board outside the grocery store and see what happened. I thought if no one claimed the kitty, then we would keep it.

I wrote, "I want to go home for Christmas" in bold letters across the top of the flyer and followed that with a description of the kitten and our phone number. A couple hours after I posted it, the telephone rang.

"It sounds just like the kitten we lost a few weeks ago. Can I come over right now?" a woman asked.

The lady and her two young daughters soon were standing on my doorstep. One of the girls gathered the kitten into her arms. "Oh, he's so cute."

The woman watched her children as they petted and cuddled the animal. "Well, it's not the cat we lost, but we would love to keep it, if that's ok with you. If the real owner calls, you can give him our number."

"That's fine. I'm sure he'll have a good home with you. Merry Christmas." I waved as they climbed back into their car with their new cat. I was happy for them, and even happier for the kitten, though I was a little disappointed that we didn't get to keep the kitty for ourselves. But soon Mark arrived, and thoughts of owning a cat quickly faded.

Years passed, and I was caring for more than enough critters. I rarely thought about cats. A few neighbors owned cats, but we rarely saw them because Susie let them know they were not welcome. Then one hot day in July, a couple years after the tornado, I heard incessant barking and primeval shrieking coming from outside. I rushed to see what was causing the dreadful commotion.

Susie had treed a cat. The animal had run up an oak tree that stood on the far side of the front lawn. It was perched on the first branch, over thirty feet up, hissing and yowling at Susie, who was dancing around the base of the tree.

"Susie! Bad dog, you leave that cat alone!"

Susie stopped barking and gave me her characteristic, sad-eyed guilty look. She stuck her tail between her legs and crept away. It was an act put on for my benefit. The truth was that she did not feel the slightest bit of remorse.

After Susie disappeared, the cat quieted, and I called up to it in a sweet, calming voice. "Kitty, kitty, come on down. Come on, sweetie, I won't hurt you. Kitty, kitty."

The cat clung to the branch and peered down at me. It did not move an inch. Even from a distance I could tell it was an enormously fat cat. It had long gray fur and one of those unnaturally flat, squashed faces that are prized by some breeders of Persian cats—an aristocrat cat. Someone had paid money for this animal.

"Kitty, kitty, come on, kitty."

"Meeee-oooww." It was a pitiful plea for help.

I walked back into the house and saw Lou coming out of his office.

"Susie has chased a cat up one of the big oaks. It's up really high. I'm not sure it can get down."

Lou snorted. "Oh, I'm sure it can get down. Don't worry about it."

But the cat remained in the tree and let out long, piteous yowls for the remainder of the day. Where was the owner of this cat? Surely its cries could be heard through the woods and across the valley. The sun was setting, and I walked out and looked up at the cat again. Maybe under cover of darkness the cat would feel secure enough to come down.

The next morning I looked out the window and sighed. This was going to be a problem. I opened the front door.

"Susie! Get away from there!"

Susie was sitting quietly at the base of the tree, gazing up at the cat. She turned to look at me. Protest was in her eyes.

But I'm not barking. I was just looking to see how the cat is doing.

"Go on! Get away from that cat!"

Susie, begrudgingly, crept away.

"Kitty, kitty, come on. Don't you know how to get down? Come on. I won't let Susie hurt you."

"Meee-oooww. Meee-eee-ooowwww."

I stood with my head craned upward, thinking. We didn't own a ladder that would come close to the cat. I went back into the house. I found Lou in his office.

"The cat is still in the tree. We are going to have to do something."

Lou swung around in his swivel chair and gave me a withering glare. "Look, Deborah. (Lou always calls me Deb except when he is angry at me.) All that cat has to do is back down. It'll figure that out once it gets hungry enough."

"I don't know." I grumbled as I went back toward the kitchen.

As the hours stretched into the hot July afternoon, my concern increased. The cat had been up there well over twenty-four hours without food or water. A thunderstorm hit in the early evening. Lightning flashed and sheets of rain poured out of the sky, and I wondered if the cat would finally find a way out of the tree.

Day three arrived, and the cat still clung to the tree, perched upon its lofty branch. It continued to let out heart-wrenching calls for help, but its cry was weakening and becoming hoarse. I hoped the cat had been able to obtain a little water from the previous evening's rain.

Lou was leaving for a business trip, and as he kissed me goodbye, he still insisted the cat could take care of itself. But I was convinced the cat was never going to come down. Unless we did something, my children and I were going to suffer the horror of watching the cat die in our tree. Then the poor kitty corpse would fall to the ground, and

I would have to bury it. Or even worse, the body wouldn't fall but would remain clamped onto the branch. The soft parts would stink and rot away, leaving the bare bones to watch over my front yard, while the years passed and the tree slowly swallowed the skeleton. There it would linger to haunt us, and forevermore we would hear eerie cat calls in the night.

Even Susie seemed worried. By now, whenever I walked outside, she would run to the base of the tree and look up, then run to me, then back to the tree. She knew something was wrong, and she expected me to fix the mess she had made.

I decided it was time to make some phone calls. First, I called the fire department. I had some nostalgic notion in my head that the local fire squad would rush to my house to rescue the cat. I had seen plenty of human interest stories on television about heroic efforts to save animals. It wouldn't take any heroism to rescue this one—a good extension ladder or a bucket truck would do the job.

The person I talked to at the fire department laughed at me. "Ma'am, we don't do that sort of thing. We can't tie up our resources rescuing some cat when we may get a call from a person who needs help."

I pleaded with the man. "I live five minutes from the fire department. You could leave here and get to your call just about as fast as you could from the station."

"No, I'm sorry. We can't help you." The person was still chuckling. I bet if it was his cat stuck up in the tree, he wouldn't have thought it was so funny,

Next, I called the Shelby County Humane Society. No one there could help, but they suggested I call a tree cutting service. The tree cutters informed me that they were not in the business of rescuing animals.

And so the cat remained trapped upon the tree limb. Day four. Day five. Six, seven, eight days passed. Eventually, the mournful animal ceased its pitiful cries for help, and it simply endured. A couple times a day I would take the garden hose and squirt water up toward the cat in an effort to keep it alive, but I knew it couldn't last much longer.

On day nine I talked to George, my brother, on the telephone. I had mentioned the cat to him shortly after the whole episode began, and now I told him the cat was still in the tree.

"Nine days? Nine days!" He was aghast. My brother was an animal lover. "I've got an extension ladder that will reach up to thirty feet. I'm coming over to get that cat down."

"I don't know, George. The cat's really high. Thirty feet may not be enough."

"It'll reach. I'm on my way."

I hung up the phone with some trepidation, but about an hour later George pulled up in his pickup truck. I greeted him, and we walked over to see the cat. We pondered the feline's situation. Great golden eyes opened in the middle of a formless mass of gray fur. The animal looked down at us for a moment, then shut its eyes again, slipping back into its dream state.

"I can reach it," George said firmly. Maybe by saying it, he hoped to make it true.

He wrestled the extension ladder out of his truck and carried it over to the big oak. He positioned it firmly on the ground and leaned it against the tree, then let it out to its fullest extension. We looked at each other.

The ladder was too short, at least a good six feet too short.

There is a character trait that runs strong in my family. My brother George inherited it in good measure. In its different manifestations it may be known as concentration, tenacity, perseverance, stick-to-itiveness. My father, whose own stubbornness was legendary, called it bullheadedness.

"Got to elevate the ladder just a few feet," George said optimistically.

"How are you going to do that?"

"Put it in the back of the pickup."

"Do what?"

I watched incredulously as George backed his truck across the lawn until it was only a couple feet from the base of the oak tree. Then he proceeded to lift the ladder and place its feet in the bed of the pickup.

The top of the ladder was still several feet short of the cat.

"George, this is not going to work, but you're so good to have come all this way to try."

"I'm not giving up. We've just got to find some way to get this ladder up higher. I've got a piece of plywood here in the truck. Don't you have some sawhorses? I could put the plywood across the sawhorses to make a platform for the ladder."

Soon George was sweating profusely as he hauled one of the heavy sawhorses out of my hot attic, then lugged it down the stairs, out the door, and across the lawn. Then he went back for the second one. The sawhorses fit perfectly in the bed of the pickup. He topped them with the half-inch thick slab of plywood. Once more he lifted the ladder, this time setting its feet upon the homemade platform. The top of the ladder was just short of the big limb that held the cat.

"That'll do."

Triumphant, George braced the feet of the ladder with some heavy blocks, then fearlessly started the climb. He had gone a few feet when the absurdity of the situation hit me. He was going to fall. I knew he was going to fall, and I would call 911, and the rescue squad from the local fire department, who wouldn't rescue the cat, would nonetheless be happy to come and attend to my broken brother.

"George, I think you should come down. I'll feel extremely horrible if you fall and kill yourself. This is too dangerous."

George must have had similar thoughts, because his voice was grim, laced with the hard edge of determination. "Well, I'm already up here."

Never looking down, George climbed all the way up until he was standing just beneath the very top of the ladder. With his left hand gripping the ladder, he reached his right hand out toward the cat. His fingers were a few inches short. He whispered sweet, soft words to the animal as he tried once more, extending his body, stretching his joints. I held my breath and prayed. Abruptly, he lurched precariously sideways, then regained his balance on the ladder.

His right hand was tightly clutching a limp clump of gray fur from which shone two big golden eyes.

"Mee-ooww."

I breathed again and cheered as George backed down the ladder. A motion in the woods caught my eyes. It was Susie, who had been watching the whole affair. When she saw me looking at her, she turned and ran away.

Just about the time my brother's feet were touching solid earth again, Lou, returning home from his business trip, came up the driveway in his black Thunderbird. He slowed the vehicle and took in the sight of George's truck with the extension ladder resting on the rickety platform made of plywood and sawhorses. He didn't quite come to a complete halt, but for a long moment he gaped at us: George, the cat, and myself. Wordless, Lou finally managed a wave before he eased on around the house to the carport in back.

We all gathered in the laundry room. The cat was in surprisingly good condition. He'd had abundant fat stores before the ordeal began, and now under the mass of fur he still had a bit of padding on his frame. The animal drank some water but just scowled at the dog food we put in front of him. He turned his head away when I stroked his fur.

"What are we were going to do with him?"

This was somebody's pampered house pet. The sun was setting, and George soon departed. His family already had enough cats. He had no desire to take this one, even though he had risked his life to save him. The cat would stay with us at least overnight.

Lou left to get cat supplies. The boys peeked at the cat but weren't very impressed. Nobody was begging to keep this animal. He had no personality.

"He's exhausted and hungry. Once he gets a full belly and a few nights sleep, he will perk up," I told the boys.

Lou came back with kitty litter and expensive gourmet cat food. The cat had a haughty attitude. He sniffed at the cat food, considering, then began to slowly eat it without a hint of purr to express gratitude. Ignoring us, he finally curled up on some towels for much needed sleep.

Had we acquired our first cat? A Sambo-type tomcat would have fit into our family much better than this coddled creature, whose main aptitude probably was for eating. I thought I would put out some flyers, and hopefully his owners would see one.

The next morning our neighbor Betty called. Betty was a great neighbor. In her younger days she had been a lovely and talented pianist. She was once a finalist in the Miss Alabama pageant, and she often served as a judge for local beauty contests. She occasionally roped Lou into helping to judge some of the high school pageants, and now he could talk with authority about the proper way to walk in high heels and an evening gown. Betty always remembered my boys' birthdays, and she frequently brought us coupons or interesting stories she clipped from the newspaper. Every Christmas she gave me a gardening book. Our dogs also looked forward to seeing her, because she brought them tasty scraps to eat. They would go wild and jump for joy when they saw her coming up the steps to the patio. Betty was a widow. Harris, her husband, had been a grandfatherly figure who had befriended Sam. He was dying of cancer the week that Sam was in the hospital so very ill with diabetes. The day Sam came home from the hospital, he went next door and briefly visited with Harris, who was at home under hospice care. Harris died the next day. That was a tough week for us all.

Betty had been talking to someone in the mountainous subdivision on the other side of the valley behind our house. This person knew someone farther up in that neighborhood who was missing a gray cat. More phone calls were made, and soon a man and woman showed up to claim their pet, whose name was Smokey.

"Our house is on the market. The realtor has been bringing lots of people through. We thought somebody looking at the house had stolen him. He's never been outside before, and we can't imagine how he got all the way down here."

I thought about Smokey, confronted with the strange, wide world for the first time, and running into Susie. Poor kitty. I explained that Smokey had climbed a tall tree and had been stuck there for nine days. I omitted details of what made the cat climb the tree in the first place, but I described how my brother had rescued him, hinting at George's gallantry. I was surprised when they did not at least ask for his number so they could call to thank him. In fact, they did not comment on George's bravery at all.

As the woman cuddled Smokey and talked, Susie came around the corner of the house and headed toward us.

Oh, no.

I could foresee the awful scene about to occur, with a shrieking cat leaping from its owner's arms and, with our dog in hot pursuit, racing to the safety of the oak tree. But I was wrong. Before I could say or do anything, Susie had politely taken her place at my side. She sat and wagged her tail in a friendly greeting and exuded good manners. *Who me? Chase a cat? No way!*

The cat looked at Susie with no hint of fear. Apparently, sometime during the past nine days Smokey and Susie had made their peace with one another. All of us, animals and people together, heaved a huge collective sigh of relief as Smokey and family got into their car and drove away.

So Smokey wasn't the cat for us, but I still thought one day it could happen. I envisioned Lou in his old age, sitting back in his lounge chair, his feet propped up. He would be taking an afternoon snooze, with a hint of a smile on his face and with a cat curled up on his lap, purring...

CHAPTER TEN
MISS PEPPER

Susie began to slow down when she was about eleven years old. One morning as she was relaxing on the patio, I watched a squirrel scamper safely in front of her, passing barely five feet in front of the dog's face. Susie's eyes followed the squirrel, but she seemed too tired to so much as raise her head. Then she noticed that I was looking at her. Clearly embarrassed to be caught neglecting her responsibilities, she hopped up to pursue the squirrel, but her heart wasn't in it. Soon she was back in her spot, her nose resting upon her front paws.

Another time, I came up the road in my car and saw Susie stretched out in front of me. She recently had taken to napping in the middle of the driveway. She lifted her head for a moment and glanced at the approaching vehicle. Then she sighed heavily, and her head flopped back onto the asphalt.

Why do you have to come through here now? Can't you see I'm trying to sleep?

I halted the minivan to wait patiently for her to haul herself up, but she continued to lie on the pavement. When she wouldn't budge, I resorted to honking the horn. Susie raised her head again and glowered at me, irritated. She clearly had no regard for human right-of-way.

I put the vehicle in park and climbed out. "Susie! You shouldn't sleep in the road. Now move it!"

At last she grudgingly shifted herself into a standing position and began to walk away, slowly and with exaggerated emphasis on the pain I was causing her arthritic joints.

But Susie wasn't stupid. She knew that neither Lou nor I would run her over, but she had no such confidence in other people. Once, when our oldest son was first learning to drive, Susie was lounging on the driveway as Sam and I slowly approached in the car. She half opened her eyes and lifted her head just enough to see who was coming. Then she jerked herself up as she recognized the person in the driver's seat: the wild child, the one who tirelessly stalked woodland animals, the hyperactive little boy who roamed the valley with stick in hand. Something was wrong! The world had tilted and overturned the comfortable order of things. As Susie bounded out of the way with renewed agility, her wide-eyed expression clearly asked me how I had allowed such a thing to happen. I wasn't sure about that myself.

I was concerned. Susie was spending an increasing amount of each day dozing, apparently losing interest in her usual activities. Was she starting the long slide into senility? I sighed. How sad that old age should rob her of her snappy spirit. Then one afternoon in

June, when the hot sticky breath of summer was settling over us, Lou came inside and mentioned that Ed and Pat had a new pup.

"It looks like a Lab. Cute. Probably about two months old. Susie is out there playing with it."

I walked down the drive toward the neighboring house and smiled. I was happy to see Susie cavorting around with a little black doggie. The two of them were yelping and chasing each other like a couple of children playing tag. So Susie's problem wasn't senility—it was loneliness. She had always socialized well with other dogs. Maybe she needed companionship with her own kind. Old people who are surrounded by friends and family usually do better than loners, so maybe that was true of dogs as well. Shepherd had been gone for years, and my three boys were growing up. They were busy with school and social activities. They often spoke to Susie or gave her a quick pat on the head, but they rarely took time to play with her. I watched her and her young friend, and I was glad our neighbors had a new pet.

The next day I saw Ed and asked him about his puppy.

He shook his head. "She doesn't belong to us. We saw her with Susie and thought she belonged to you."

Uh, oh.

I looked to where Susie was rooting around in the shrubs near the edge of the woods. Sure enough, she had a small black shadow at her side.

"Come, Susie," I called.

Susie came, and so did her shadow. But the puppy stayed back about ten feet, refusing to come closer. She was black, except for an irregularly shaped white blaze on her chest and white markings on her feet that made her appear as if she had been walking through white paint. She was not wearing a collar. When I tried to get close to her, she backed away. She seemed healthy, but she was leery of humans.

When I fed Susie later that day, the little dog watched from the other side of the patio. She eyed Susie's food and crept a few feet closer. However, although she desperately wanted something to eat, she skittered away as soon as I turned in her direction. I held out some scraps and called to her softly. Several times she came toward me, then danced away again. I tossed the food onto the concrete a few feet in front of me. She crouched down with her nose resting on her front paws and gazed longingly at the food. Then, dragging her belly like a soldier in enemy territory, she slowly pulled herself forward until she got within inches of the tasty morsels. But at the last moment she glanced up at me and then dashed away, back to the safe spot on the other side of the patio. She continued to watch me warily until I turned and went into the house. When I looked out the window, she was wolfing down the scraps.

"You know," I told Lou, "I don't think that dog has been around people at all. She acts wild. I think somebody must have thrown her out on the side of the road as soon as she was weaned from her mother. She certainly has attached herself to Susie."

It was good to see Susie being her old self again, young at heart as she introduced the newcomer to her surroundings. Lou and I considered the responsibilities of another dog: feeding, training, health care, socialization, and other important obligations that come with pet ownership. The puppy seemed to have a good temperament, despite her shyness. We decided for Susie's benefit that we would adopt the puppy if we could get her to accept human contact.

I took the domestication of the little dog as my personal challenge. I was going to make her love me.

I began preparing food for the puppy every time I fed Susie. At first I put her food bowl on the far side of the patio, then returned to the house so that she could eat without being stressed by my presence. After a couple of days, I put the bowl down in the usual spot, but then I sat down in a chair near the kitchen door to watch her while she ate. She eyed me suspiciously as she slowly approached the food. She ate quickly, keeping a distrustful eye on me while she gobbled the food. But she ate her next feeding with barely a glance in my direction. Each day over the next week, foot by foot, I placed her food bowl closer to where I sat. Then one evening I placed the container right beside my feet. She was wary at first, considering the situation from a distance. After a few moments, she made up her mind. She approached and began eating with only an occasional quick peek up toward me. The next morning I held a piece of meat in my hand and reached out to her.

Visibly trembling, the puppy cautiously inched toward my outstretched hand. Still standing back a couple of feet, she advanced toward my fingertips by extending her neck out as far as it could possibly be stretched. She pulled her lips back and carefully used the very tips of her teeth to pull the tidbit out of my hand. Then she bolted to the other side of the patio before she swallowed it.

"Good girl! See, I won't hurt you. You are such a good doggie. What a precious, beautiful puppy you are."

My praise was gooey sweet, and she rewarded me by wagging her tail. I held out another scrap, and this time she came forward and took it from my hand with almost no hesitation.

I smiled. I was winning.

A few hours later I was sitting on the steps by the patio when Susie came up to me. I reached over and gave her a hug and began to stroke her under the chin. In a flash there was a movement from the side, and a little black body was pushing its way between Susie and me, wanting some similar attention for itself. Susie sat back and grinned approval as I loved on the newest member of our family.

I had won.

The boys had observed my efforts to befriend the puppy, and one of their first responsibilities had been to give her a name. They decided to call her Miss Pepper, because she had so much energy and because she "pepped up" Susie. I was eager to tell them that Miss Pepper was going to be our dog.

I picked up Mark from a friend's house that afternoon.

"Guess what, Mark! Miss Pepper ate out of my hand today, and she let me pet her. I think she's going to work out fine. I'm going to take her to the vet and get her shots and ID tag, so she'll be officially ours." I waited for my son's enthusiastic response.

Mark sat in the passenger seat of the car and looked glum, his arms crossed over his chest.

I glanced toward him. "What's wrong, Mark?"

He sighed.

"Mark?"

"I don't think it's a good idea for us to keep Miss Pepper."

"What? Why not? I thought you would be excited about it. Remember, we talked about adopting her. She'll be fun to play with, and she'll be a great companion for Susie."

Mark shook his head. He seemed very sad. "It won't be that way."

"What do you mean? I don't understand why you are saying that. I thought you liked her."

He shook his head again. "Something's going to happen."

"Oh, don't be silly. Everything will be fine."

Miss Pepper was a joy. The vet pronounced her healthy and told us she was about eight weeks old. We were right when we had guessed that she had been weaned recently from her mother. She was full of the mischievous enthusiasm of a young one exploring the world for the first time. We all laughed at her antics as she bounced after Susie. Her ears flapped as she twirled to chase bugs, and her tail wagged energetically as she pursued ground squirrels.

She had a sweet disposition, but she played a tough game of tug-of-war. When she latched onto her end of a towel, no earthly force could move her to release her grip. This small puppy had the jaws of a Tyrannosaurus rex. Susie would play a while, holding valiantly onto her end as Miss Pepper assaulted the other side, until Susie grew tired of the game. Then Miss Pepper would bounce toward me with the towel, taunting me to grab the other end. Soon I also would grow tired, and still Miss Pepper wanted to play. One day she discovered the thick climbing rope hanging down from the children's old swing set. She attacked this rope relentlessly, growling and jerking it backwards until she was pulled off her feet. The thick wooden beam that held the other end of the rope never grew tired.

She liked to go on walks down the drive, trotting beside me, with little excursions into the woodland border to check out interesting attractions. There is a fire hydrant near the end of the road, next to the drive where it rises over a slight elevation before curving down toward the main highway. The first time Miss Pepper saw the short, stubby cylinder, she halted in her tracks and glared at it. She backed up and emitted a low growl, crouching down and refusing to go a step farther. Did she have bad memories associated with that spot? Did someone toss her out beside the fire hydrant, abandoning her there to fend for herself? I didn't push her. It was good stopping point, because beyond the fire hydrant was a view of the highway, which was an evil place for a puppy to go. We turned around and headed back toward the house.

Before long we all lay low under the torrid days of high summer. Plants wilted as the intense heat sucked moisture out of the ground—and out of people too, drawing long streams of sweat from the face and neck and other body parts of anyone forced to work outside. I retreated into the air conditioned comfort of the house and searched the skies for signs of rain, while Susie and Miss Pepper curled up and slept through the heat within depressions they dug in the cool earth beneath shrubs. I was ready for July and August to be done.

"Miss Pepper will have so much fun this fall," I told my family.

I imagined her pleasure amidst piles of fallen leaves. We would explore the forest once the weeds and bugs diminished, and I thought about teaching her some tricks. Maybe there would be some snow this winter. She would enjoy that.

September arrived, and during the first hours after dawn there was a little nip in the air, which succumbed to rising temperatures by mid-morning but, nevertheless, promised the coming of autumn. The children were back in school. Sam was in the tenth grade, Josh in the ninth, and Mark in the fifth. High school football games were the popular outing on Friday nights, where if the favorite team lost, the fans on either side would comfort themselves by the fact that their school had the better band. On Saturdays, sustained chants of "Roll Tide!" and "War Eagle!" reverberated across the state as masses packed into stadiums to watch our college teams, while multitudes of others ordered in pizza and watched the games on television. Grocery stores featured deep red and mellow golden apples, and fat orange pumpkins and colorful decorative gourds appeared at roadside stands. Dogwood trees began to show a blush of pink in their leaves. Department stores displayed fall and winter clothing, although the weather remained much too warm to wear most of it. People began to plant mums and other fall flowers in their yards.

One Wednesday morning I was driving home from a women's Bible study at the church. The atmosphere was damp from recent rain, but some bluish patches were showing through broken gray clouds. It was almost noon, and my mind had shifted from spiritual matters to lunch. I was a few hundred feet from the turn off the highway onto our road when a white flash ahead caught my eye.

It was Susie. I watched, appalled, as she dashed across the highway, traveling from the wooded area on the left, back toward our side of the road. She made it safely and continued over a huge grassy field, headed in the direction of our house. She never slowed down or looked back.

I had not seen Susie near this highway, ever. The fence around the dog yard had been destroyed by the tornado, but pressed with many other expenses, we had never replaced it. Susie had always been content to roam the acres of woods and valley adjacent to our home. She never wandered away or bothered the neighbors. There was minimal traffic on the one lane road which meandered back into our small corner of Helena, so we didn't worry about it. She once had a close call with a UPS truck, and since then she had maintained a healthy respect for trucks and cars. I was concerned about Miss Pepper when we first adopted her, but she, even more so than Susie, seemed to have an instinctive fear of all vehicles on the road. Sensible dog.

Miss Pepper.

Immediately after Susie had safely crossed the highway, I saw a little black dog emerge from the woods, following after her. At that very moment a car was coming over a slight rise in the highway.

"Oh, no!" I was stricken. At a distance I could see what was about to happen.

Miss Pepper hesitated at the edge of the road, and in that fraction of a second I desperately hoped she would see the oncoming car. But she was looking after Susie, and she made a big joyous leap directly into the path of the car. The car knocked her up into the air with a violent thud that tore apart my heart. She was killed instantly.

Dazed, I pulled over and got out of the car. I had to get her out of the middle of the road before any more cars ran over her. The young woman who hit her also stopped. She was distraught as she came to where I was moving Miss Pepper to the shoulder of the road.

"I didn't see it. It just jumped right in front of me."

"It's not your fault. There's no way you could have avoided her." My voice was trembling.

"I wonder who it belongs to."

"Me. She's my dog. She belongs to me."

She shook her head, clearly shocked. "Oh! I'm so sorry! Do you need some help?"

"No, I'm fine. I can take care of everything. It's OK."

After more apologies the woman departed. Leaving Miss Pepper beside the drive, I drove to the house. I found an old blanket, then returned and wrapped her in it. Her spine had been crushed, but there wasn't much blood—most of the injuries were internal. As horrible as it was, I was grateful that I had been there to see how it happened. I knew she hadn't suffered, and I was thankful that I was able to move her before additional traffic could mutilate her body.

I laid Miss Pepper in the cargo section of the minivan and carried her home. I was shaken to my core. I wanted to bury her before I had to pick the boys up from school, as if I could cover up the awful thing that had happened. I dreaded having to tell them that Miss Pepper was dead. I didn't want them to see her. Especially Mark. I felt so guilty. We should have replaced the fence.

I gently positioned her body in a wheelbarrow and then found a shovel. Lou was not home, so this was my responsibility. Darkening clouds were filling up the sky again, and there were a few sprinkles as I rolled her down into the yard. I called Susie, who was off in the woods somewhere, because I wanted her to know what had happened. I was mad at Susie.

"Susie! Susie! Come here, Susie!"

Susie didn't come. Tears began to flow down my face, but I made no effort to wipe them away. There was no point in it. The rain increased as I began digging a hole near a Japanese maple tree, and the tears and the rain mingled together and dripped off my chin. I thrust the shovel into the damp red clay, and I was grateful that the day's rain had softened the earth.

I began to think about death. I have known people who died: old people, children, people my own age, relatives, and friends. I have seen people of all ages die in the hospital, despite the medical team's desperate efforts to shock their hearts back to life. And there was the tiniest of all, my own unborn child who was known only to me as a small flutter that never fulfilled its promise.

Death is such a tragedy. People may slip quietly into the night, or they may go forth with wrenching passion and agonized protests. They may face death bravely, head on, or perhaps they never face death at all but are caught from behind, unawares. But whatever the circumstances of death and however we cover it over with euphemisms and surround it with ceremony, our hearts rebel against it.

I once heard our world compared to a magnificent cathedral that had been bombed during a war. The great stone walls of the soaring structure may take your breath away, but there is no roof. You may admire the colors of stained glass windows, until you notice jagged holes in the glass and step upon the sharp edges of shards beneath your feet. Although the building gives evidence of its former glory, what remains of its beauty points to the heartbreak of its destruction.

The bombs still fall upon our world. Even the most valiant and strongest among us become exhausted by the constant struggle to hold back the evil forces that endeavor to destroy what is good. Children suffer abuse and starvation, and people die in car wrecks and earthquakes and fires. Innocent individuals are blown apart by the weapons of terrorists, and soldiers march to war to kill each other. Gangs roam inner cities and brutally assassinate members of rival gangs, unconcerned if they catch bystanders in the crossfire. Mothers in the prime of their lives die of cancer. Grandfathers are stricken down by heart attacks. Healthy young people are doomed to grow old, wither, and then to die. It is all wrong. Death is the enemy. The earth is held captive, and each individual tragedy is a symptom of a fallen, broken world crying out for salvation.

I worked to enlarge the hole, heaping the sticky red clay to the side.

What about the ladies' Bible study? I'm a Christian. Isn't the world's struggle with evil and death what the Bible is all about? Those holy pages surely offer comfort and hope in the face of hardship, disaster, and grief, with firm promises that what is wrong will one day be made right.

My shovel hit a big rock, stuck in the ground. I wedged the shovel under a corner of the stone and pushed hard to dislodge it from the bloodshot soil. Amidst the crush of all the world's agony, what is the death of one small dog?

Certainly, no detail is beneath God's attention. His work is evident in mighty constellations following their paths in perfect order and also in astonishing worlds of infinite smallness. We may look up and wonder at the stars, but most of us go about our daily business and never think of the teeming life that exists on hidden levels all around us and inside us and underneath us. Can we grasp a world where ants work together like a living computer network to process information from the world above them, or where plants communicate with insects by using chemical signals? Can we fathom that a single handful of earth contains billions of bacteria living within their own intricate world? Do we have any inkling of how all nature is designed to work together to promote life and well-being throughout the earth, and do we understand how often we humans carelessly upset this symbiosis?

When I was a child I saw a film in class about diatoms, tiny one-celled life forms that dwell in the depths of the ocean, far from human eyes. I still remember the complex, stunningly beautiful configurations of those microscopic bits of algae. And I remember the film's narrator asking the question, "For whose eyes was such beauty created?" Since then I have had a greater appreciation for tiny things, and one of my favorite courses in college was microbiology. I once saw a bit of slime under the microscope. To my eyes the stuff looked snotty and gross, but high magnification revealed its true nature to be exquisite artwork—those diatoms again.

Scientists with powerful microscopes are beginning to explore this vast universe in the realm of the invisible. The deeper they go, the more sophisticated the discoveries. The "simple" cell is a factory of life, more complex than the computers that sent men to the moon, and molecular biologists are astounded by the language of DNA contained within each cell, with chemical words, sentences, and paragraphs telling each cell how to grow.

I placed Miss Pepper in a hole in the earth and covered her shattered body with soil. Did the God of the Universe take note of it? Jesus said that not a single sparrow falls to the ground apart from God, so I cannot believe that I was alone as I buried this one of God's humble creatures.

I told the boys on the way home from school. Mark, sitting in the back seat, shook his head.

"I knew it. I knew it. I told you something would happen."

"You were right, Mark. I'm so sorry."

Later that sad day as the fading sun descended beneath the fingers of the night, Susie sat in front of the house, gazing steadfastly across the lawn toward the highway. As far as I know, she never again went near there. As for me, for a long time I would have the most irrational urge: a desire to dig up Miss Pepper to make sure she was really dead.

I so badly wanted things to be different.

CHAPTER ELEVEN

JASMINE AND LILY

I took Mark to the dentist for an adjustment of his braces one afternoon the year after Miss Pepper had died. Many of the children from Mark's school used this dentist's services, and the waiting room was crowded. Colorful artwork and photos taken at high school football games covered the walls. A child's table in one corner held toys to entertain smaller children, and a couple of preschoolers were playing in that area. Near the door a little boy snuggled in his mother's lap as she read aloud to him. A selection of magazines covered a large rectangular coffee table in the middle of the room, and a few adults sat in chairs looking at these while they waited. Some teenagers were working on homework. Soft music played in the background.

Mark and I stopped to sign in at the receptionist's desk. As I was writing, I noticed a photograph propped up on the counter. The image featured black Labrador retriever puppies spilling out of a big basket.

"Oh, Mark! Aren't they cute?"

As I viewed the picture, my heart melted. "And that one looks just like Miss Pepper."

A puppy in the front of the basket had a white blaze on its chest and a lively expression on its face. I eyed the "For Sale" sign that accompanied the picture and hardened my mushy heart. "But we can't get another puppy. We don't have a fence, and you know I said we would not get another dog until we had a fence."

My son rolled his eyes in response. So far he had not participated in this conversation.

We joined the others in the waiting area, and in a few minutes an assistant called Mark back to see the dentist. I dug through the pile of magazines to find something to read while I waited. But soon I was gazing back toward the picture. Susie was very old now, and after she was gone there would be no more dogs at our place. On the other hand, there was the matter of the fence.

I told myself to forget it. We didn't need another animal.

When Mark and I arrived home, I immediately began telling Lou about the puppies.

"There is a litter of black Lab puppies for sale. You should see the picture of them. They're all in a basket, and they are the cutest things. One of them looks just like Miss Pepper, with the white mark on its chest. Oh, I know we're not getting another dog. We need that like a hole in the head. But they sure are cute. I mean, we can't have another dog. We don't have a fence, and I said we aren't getting any more dogs unless we have a fence. But that one in the front of the basket does look just like Miss Pepper. You should see it."

Lou fixed his eyes on me. "Well, you know we could get a fence."

"Really? You mean it?"

"Sure. I bet Mr. Simpson could put us one up in no time."

Mr. Simpson was a carpenter who over the years had done many projects around our house. He currently was doing some work on the carport. We first hired him to install a skylight in the upstairs bathroom we added to our house after the tornado. He was a wiry, middle-aged man with a beard, a motorcycle, and five children. We liked him. He was honest, dependable, and did good work. When he was working at our house, he made us feel like he really wanted to be there and that he was working only for us, although we knew he was a busy man with many other customers. I sometimes have hired people who flat-out let me know what a favor they were doing for me by consenting to squeeze me into their hectic schedules. They would work a little bit on my project, then rush off to hit a lick for somebody else, and eventually they might come back and hit another lick for me. Such workers have made me appreciate a man like Mr. Simpson. Sometimes when we called him, he would tell us that he was currently working on a big job and that we would have to wait a few weeks. We usually didn't mind waiting.

If we were going to have a dog yard, I wanted it to be attractive. I didn't want a metal chain link fence like the original one. (Oh, no. That wouldn't do. The look of the fence trumped practicality.) I held an idyllic image of a picket fence in my mind. So I talked to Mr. Simpson about putting one up adjacent to the back side of the house where the office is located. I didn't know that some dogs eat wood.

I called to ask about the puppies. They would be ready to leave their mother the next week, and I was glad to hear that the one with the white blaze was a female. I wanted a female, because male dogs have the bad habit of hiking their legs and spraying plants in the garden. On a hot summer day, that's as good as using an herbicide.

I decided to name the new puppy Jasmine. I told Mr. Simpson about the Labrador puppy and the date I would need the fence to be finished, and he promised to have it completed by then. I sat and watched him as he began cutting wood for the fence, and I chatted away about the upcoming addition to our family. I didn't pretend that I was getting a puppy for the children. This doggie was going to be mine.

Mr. Simpson worked late into the evening the day before I was to get Jasmine. We had to turn on the floodlights for him to see as he worked on the finishing touches. I was pleased with the results. The fence was four feet tall, and a decorative gothic style arch topped each picket. I thought it considerably improved the view of that side of the house. I envisioned flowers growing outside the dog yard along the base of the new fence, including a climbing rose that would grow up and spread outward across the top.

The next morning I drove out to the dentist's home, tucked away in the woods at the end of a twisty drive. His wife greeted me warmly, and we followed a path to the back yard. She opened the gate to a dog yard, and eight little jumping balls of black fur tumbled out and bounced off in different directions.

"Come here, puppies!"

Almost all of the puppies ignored the call, but one skidded to a stop, turned, and then raced back toward us. I knelt down, and it leaped into my arms.

"Oh, you're so smart," I praised the puppy as I looked it over.

This wasn't the one with the white blaze on the chest, but it was a female. She was solid black except for a sprinkling of white hairs on the chin. Her fur was wondrously soft, thick and fluffy, and felt baggy, for her skin was a little too big for her bones. She snuggled in my lap and looked up at me with shining brown eyes as I petted her. There was complete trust and adoration in her look. This animal had never known anything but love. I put her down and watched her bound away to join her siblings.

I observed the one with the white blaze. She was the wild brat of the bunch, darting around, attacking the environment and jumping on her mother. Mama dog was very patient as her baby chewed on her legs and ears, but I was concerned about how elderly Susie might respond.

I called the first puppy back to me. She came immediately, and again she contentedly cuddled in my lap as I scratched behind her ears and under her chin. This would always be one of her favorite things to do, even when she had grown to over seventy pounds and her haunches and long legs overflowed my lap and spilled onto the ground.

So it was that I did not choose Jasmine, but Jasmine chose me. I'm pleased to report that the puppy with the white blaze also found a home—with Mr. Simpson the carpenter, who was so smitten with Jasmine when he saw her that he went to get a puppy for his own family. They named her Bambi.

Jasmine was a good addition to our household. To the end of her days, Susie was alert and intelligent, and she was a terrific grandma. She relished the youthful antics of her new companion. Many mornings I would hear noises coming from the dog yard, and when I looked out, I would see Jasmine and Susie rolling around and chasing each other. Susie, if she caught me watching, would give me a bemused look.

Okay, now I'm just being a good babysitter, right?

Jasmine was a prodigiously playful puppy. She was easy to train and quickly learned the basics of "sit," "stay," "come," "heel," and "bring it to me." She turned out to be a talented soccer player, chasing the ball and pushing it along the lawn with her nose. She didn't know all the official rules—in fact, our particular brand of doggie soccer didn't have any rules—but she did know how to steal the ball and keep it out of her opponent's possession. Sometimes Sam and I teamed up against her, and in the end we would find ourselves sprawled on the ground, panting and soaked with sweat, while Jasmine triumphantly peered at us from across the lawn with the soccer ball tucked neatly behind her front legs.

She also liked to play catch, but she wasn't as good at this game and rarely managed to catch the ball in midair. Most of the time she ended up chasing it as it bounced and rolled across the yard. When at last she caught up with it, she would gather it into her mouth and then return at full gallop so that I could throw it again. In the beginning I let her to drop it into my hand. But the thing usually came back to me covered with gooey slobber, so I soon taught her to "put it in the basket." I found that I could direct her to put any object into a basket, and she would hurry to do so. This trick always impressed visiting children and relatives. Another popular performance involved her attempt at playing dead. She would roll over onto her back and stick her paws in the air while letting her tongue hang out the side of her mouth, although she never held the pose quite long enough to be convincing.

Susie, Jasmine, and I got into the routine of taking a daily stroll down the road. I trained Jasmine to walk beside me, and Susie would amble along a little ahead of us, slowly, because of her stiff joints. I imagined that Jasmine would become my protector someday after Susie was gone, though I began to have doubts about this when one morning we were confronted by a trio of wild dogs.

They were big, boney, hungry-looking creatures, drooling at the mouth, with diseased skin and mongrel ancestry. They stood stiff in front of us and snarled, blocking the road where it rose over a little knoll ahead of us. My heart began to thump.

Old Susie was outnumbered and half their size. She had arthritis, and, although we didn't know it yet, cancer was beginning to grow inside her. But brave-hearted soul, she valiantly leaped forward and halted a few feet in front of the growling beasts. Her posture was rigid and defiant as she planted her feet and squared off her stance. She was ready for battle. She barked loudly and with fury. NOBODY was going to threaten her family.

Meanwhile, Jasmine, who by then had grown almost to her full adult size, nearly knocked me over as she bolted behind me, then cautiously sneaked a peek by forcefully pushing her face between my thighs. I don't know exactly what Susie told those dogs, but she convinced them that she meant business. They shut up and glared at us a moment, then turned away and headed off into the woods. I praised and petted Susie, but I had to laugh at Jasmine. Despite her bright mind and powerful body, sweet Jasmine was a coward. (I was being harsh. Jasmine, despite her size, was still only a child dog.)

Jasmine was so smart that I felt a little guilty about owning such a quality animal. I once gave her a canine IQ test I found in the *Reader's Digest*, and she scored one point below doggie genius. Professionally trained, she would have been an outstanding service dog, but her potential was wasted in our self-sufficient household.

She also could have been a great drug dog, for she had a fine nose. One day the two of us were on one of our walks. Jasmine was beside me, snuffling along the road, finding wild black cherries that had fallen off a tree. She had a taste for all sorts of fruit, and wild cherries and muscadine grapes were among her favorites. If they were overripe or slightly fermented, all the better. So she was grazing along the asphalt, searching carefully and sucking up each little shriveled cherry, with an occasional side trip to the thick woods along the side of the road to explore for Muscadine grapes, when we came to an automobile that was parked on the edge of the road in front of Ed and Pat's house. It was a nondescript car, the whitish, generic kind that blends unremarkably into the background. I would scarcely have noticed it if my dog hadn't become so excited. The vehicle did not belong to my neighbors, but I remembered seeing it parked in front of the their house on a couple of other occasions. I assumed it belonged to a relative or friend or possibly to someone who was doing some work for them.

Jasmine began to sniff the tires. Jasmine had never shown particular interest in automobiles before, but her action wasn't so unusual. Probably another dog had peed on the wheels. But then she began to focus on the metal hubcaps, quickly moving from tire to tire in a frenzy, pushing her nose against the rim, sniff-sniff-sniffing all the way around each wheel.

"Come on, Jasmine," I called.

Now she was sniffing the back of the car. She put her front paws on the bumper and pulled herself up so as to have better access as she worked her nose across the trunk and back again.

I looked around nervously, thinking about dead bodies and having anxious thoughts about drug runners and other nefarious characters. I was sure my neighbors were both upstanding members of the community, but I couldn't vouch for all of their associates.

"Jasmine! Come!"

Jasmine ignored me and proceeded to smell the hubcaps again.

"Good grief, dog, leave that car alone. Come on!"

I finally had to grab her collar and forcefully drag her away from the vehicle. At last we continued our walk, but I did wonder what was inside that car.

In Susie's last weeks, cancer began to take away her physical abilities. A few days before her death, she watched as Jasmine and I headed down the road for our walk. Slowly, she pushed herself up from the patio to join us. I observed her as she limped along. Her body was emaciated, but her eyes were still clear and expressive, her mind as sharp as ever. She seemed content.

It was a warm June morning. The sun was bright, filtering through the tree canopy, and birds and squirrels called out from amidst the leaves. We didn't go far, less than halfway down the road and back. We took our time. I looked at her, and I knew this would be our last walk together. I was sorry that I didn't have any good photographs of her. She rarely had paused long enough to get a good shot, and, well, she had always been so filthy, covered with dirt and leaves and other residue from her forays into the woods. Now I was sorry that we hadn't taken the extra effort to get a photo before she had become sick and frail. She lay on the patio when we got back to the house, and for a while I sat with her, gently petting her and remembering the good times. I was so sad. I was going to miss her.

A couple days later Lou came in and handed me a sack. Inside were photos he had taken on a recent boy scout trip. He had used an old camera that contained a partially used-up roll of film, long forgotten. (This was in the days before digital cameras. Photos were taken on rolls of film, which then had to be sent out for development.) The film was at least six years old, and he wasn't sure if the pictures would be any good.

The pictures came out fine. We admired the recent boy scout shots, then eyed some photos made years ago during the "great blizzard of '93." This was a March storm that had affected a good portion of the country. In Helena, we had watched in astonishment as winds up to forty miles an hour hurled snow at us in thick, blinding sheets that rapidly covered the earth and roads. When it was over, our yard had disappeared under snowdrifts up to four feet deep. The storm created problems for many areas throughout the region. I'll never forget televised video of a group of medics carrying a pregnant woman on a stretcher, struggling up the long hill to Brookwood Hospital in Homewood, Alabama, because the deep snow made the road impassable even to emergency vehicles.

Our mild spring temperatures had returned within a week, and all the snow had melted to expose frostbitten evergreens and deciduous shrubs whose new spring growth had been blackened. Despite the shivering plants, the new season would not be thwarted. Eager for spring, daffodil foliage bravely pushed up through the last bits of snow, and eventually the frost-nipped bushes recovered. Nevertheless, for a few magical days our house sat in the middle of a snowbound land that resembled, not the Deep South, but the pristine frozen wastelands of the Far North.

Lou and I lingered over the pictures. We marveled at our boys, now nearly grown, grinning out from the past. I smiled at them building a snowman. It was a terrific snowman with sticks for arms, a wide charcoal mouth, and Groucho Marx eyeglasses, nose, and mustache, originally purchased as part of a costume. Then tears filled my eyes. The next photo was of Susie standing between Josh and the snowman. She was in her prime, enjoying life and smiling at the camera.

The day after we got the pictures, Susie passed away quietly in her sleep. She had lived a full fourteen years, and when she died we buried her under the Japanese maple tree near Miss Pepper. She was a fine animal, and we loved her.

After Susie was gone, I tried to spend more time with Jasmine, but my time with her was never enough. She hated being penned up alone inside the dog yard. She grew into a great escape artist, and she earned the nickname "Houdini Dog." She was just tall enough to reach the fence's regular latch, and she soon mastered the task of opening it—a simple flip of her snout would do the trick—so we wound wire around the thing to keep it shut. To our amazement, she would patiently use her teeth and tongue to tug and pull on the wire until it was loose, and then it was an easy matter to unwind it and open the latch.

Most of the time she would present herself at the large sliding glass door that is located in the breakfast area of our kitchen, only about ten feet from the dog yard. I would walk into the kitchen and find her waiting for me, grinning and wagging her tail to announce her accomplishment. Then back to the dog yard she would have to go, where she would begin mapping out her next escape attempt.

The thing was, Jasmine could see most of what was going on in the kitchen through its glass doors. If Jasmine saw one of us enter the room, she would immediately stop trying to unwind the wire, because she knew she was about to be sternly admonished to halt what she was doing. She was very obedient—until we turned our backs. Then, the next time we looked around, there she would be, grinning as she sat at the kitchen door.

I said *most* of the time Jasmine came to the kitchen door when she escaped. The other times were fraught with disaster. Sometimes she came home with a mysterious shoe or garden glove, but usually she went searching for food, as if we didn't feed her enough at our house. She liked to explore our neighbors' trash cans and bring home interesting, smelly pieces of garbage. A dog is ruined once it has acquired a taste for garbage.

Construction workers were building new houses on the land that had previously pastured horses, and some of them had the practice of dumping scraps and odorous wrappings from their lunches into the surrounding woods. I eventually had to keep Jasmine on the leash when we took our walks. Otherwise, she would get a whiff of the workers' discarded goodies and would take off and be gobbling trash before I could catch her.

One time Jasmine escaped from the dog yard and ran down the road to Ed and Pat's house, where a painter was working for the day. He had left a sack with his lunch and a loaf of bread he had bought for his mother on the front seat of his pickup truck, and he also had rolled the truck's windows down to keep the inside of the cab from getting too hot. Pat gave us a call to let us know that our dog had climbed into the painter's truck and had consumed both his lunch and his mom's loaf of bread.

At last we found a big bolt for the dog yard's gate that was impossible for Jasmine to undo, but then she began to eat the fence. She was persistent, chewing off little bits of wood when we weren't watching. It was hard to catch her doing the deed, but we knew she was working on it because pieces of the fence were disappearing. She managed to make an opening in the slats large enough for a couple of paws and a good portion of her face to fit through. She would lie with her nose resting on her paws stuck through the fence, observing everything that went on in the kitchen, waiting wistfully for someone to come out to play. Having developed a liking for wood, if she was particularly bored she would eat the house, gnawing small chunks of siding off the outside wall of Lou's office. We sprayed the wood with hot sauce in an effort to discourage her, but apparently that just made the wood tastier. We ultimately had to pay a lot of money to have the siding replaced on that portion of the house.

She also began to bark. While Susie was alive, Jasmine had rarely barked, but now she discovered her voice. If I was late getting out to take her for her morning walk, she barked. If she caught sight of me inside the kitchen, she barked. She barked at me when she saw me working in the yard. When I left to run errands, she barked at my car as I drove down the road. I felt guilty when I looked out and saw her gazing at me from within the confines of the dog yard. Jasmine needed more attention than I could give her. She was discontented and lonely.

"We have to get another dog," I announced to Lou. "Jasmine can't stand being in that dog yard by herself." Lou had already come to the same conclusion, and he nodded approval.

"Yes, just go down to the animal shelter and pick one out." Neither of us wanted to spend a lot of money on another animal, and it would be good to give a home to a dog that might not otherwise survive.

That night I lay in bed, thinking. What kind of dog would I get? Probably a puppy, but one old enough to play with Jasmine, maybe around three months. What color? I remembered Susie. I had told myself I would never have another dog with long white hair that showed dirt and became matted so easily, but wouldn't a white puppy be a pretty contrast to Jasmine's shining black fur? Of course it would be a girl dog. What should I name her? Rosemary? No, if she was white, I would call her Lily. I drifted off to sleep, dreaming of frolicking white puppies.

The next day while the boys were in school, I visited one of the shelters run by the Jefferson County Humane Society. This one was located inside a shopping mall, and it looked much like a pet store. I walked around and peered into the various cages. There were several adult dogs, a few cats, and some small puppies. Most of the animals seemed dispirited and barely responded to my overtures. Some of them glanced at me through the wires of their prison, but there was no play left in them.

I sighed. Not much to choose from. One cage contained a litter of mixed shepherd-collie puppies. They were brown and black, adorable fuzzy things. They seemed very young, only a few weeks old, but I didn't see any other puppies that interested me. I was thinking about how fast a puppy grows when the lady at the desk looked my way.

"Those are too young for us to release yet. Can I help you look for something else?"

"Well, I have an adult Labrador that needs a companion. Since our other dog died, she's been lonesome. She's very playful, and I want a dog that will be a playmate for her. It has to be a female dog that can live outside. I was wanting a puppy, but one old enough to romp with my other dog. Around three months would be good."

"Hmmm...well, I don't have anything like that out here, but there is one three-month-old collie mix in the back getting a bath right now. If you want, you can go back there and take a look at her."

I followed the woman through a door into the next room. I stopped and gawked at a ponderous gray cat who sat brooding over his territory in the middle of the floor, like a thundercloud about to burst. He weighed fifty pounds, at least. He glared at me from under massive, drooping brows.

The woman must have seen my jaw drop. "That's Sumo," she said. "Everyone who comes in here wants to take him home, but we've got him on a special diet and he's not up for adoption."

She drew my attention away from Sumo and pointed to a sink in the corner where an assistant was lathering shampoo over a boney animal. Pink flesh showed through the stringy white fur that was plastered to its body. Big brown eyes dominated the pointy face. "However, Lily here needs a home badly."

My jaw dropped again. "What! What did you call her?"

"Well, we call her Lily, but if you adopt her, you're free to rename her anything you want."

"Oh, no. Lily's a great name. In fact, I had already decided that I wanted to get a white puppy and call her Lily. Oh, dear." I stared at the scrawny wet creature.

The woman and her assistant both beamed at me. "Well, then it's meant to be. I'm sure Lily will be a fine friend for your other dog. She is a very sweet animal, and she loves to play."

"Oh, my..." I walked over to get a closer look, and Lily wagged her long, soapy tail at me. She had the thin face of a collie, but otherwise it was hard to guess her ancestry.

"Here, let me get her out of this bath, so you can play with her." The assistant quickly rinsed her off and then enfolded her in a big towel. After she patted her with the towel for a few minutes, she reached for a hair dryer.

Lily was pleased with all the attention. She sat still, and her eyes glowed as the assistant waved the blow dryer over her body. I gazed in wonderment as the wet, stringy fur turned into a downy cloud of white fluff.

"There you go!" The assistant finished and put the puppy on the floor.

Lily bounded over toward Sumo. She yelped as she danced about the cat, bowing down, then leaping backwards, enticing the cat to play. Sumo contemplated the maker of all this commotion and then lowered his thick lids until his green eyes were glowering out through thin slits. Sumo had not moved an inch since I entered the room.

"See what I mean? Lily really does need a playmate." The lady from the front desk watched me. "You just take your time getting to know her. I'll be out front when you get ready to do the paperwork."

"Come here, Lily," I called.

The puppy came to me at once and bounced into my arms. There was no hesitation on her part at all. She was ready to go home. After I paid the adoption fee and filled out all the forms, I took Lily out to the car and put her in the large cardboard box I had placed on the passenger side of the front seat. As I drove home, she sat tall in the box so she could see out the window. She watched the traffic lights and other sights with interest. She moved her head back and forth as trucks, cars, buildings, and trees sped by. There was a guy on a bicycle. She occasionally glanced over toward me and grinned. She was altogether satisfied with the situation.

I had some trepidation as I pulled up to the house. What if Jasmine didn't like her? What if she was jealous?

"Well, here you are, Lily," I announced as I opened the car door and gathered the puppy into my arms. "Come on, lets go meet your sister." I hugged her to my chest as I carried her around the house to the dog yard.

Jasmine was lying beside the doghouse when she saw me. She jumped up and ran toward the fence, wagging her tail. Lily began wiggling in my arms and tried to leap into the dog yard.

"Here you go, Jasmine. This is your new puppy!"

I bent over and dropped Lily into the fresh pine straw that covered the dog yard. The two animals greeted each other with unrestrained joy.

"Jasmine!"

"Lily!"

It was as if they were long-lost best friends. They leaped and rolled and chased each other until they were both spent, and when they had played themselves out they curled up together inside the doghouse.

Lily grew up to be same size as Jasmine. We decided that she had some bird dog in her, because of some telltale spots on her legs and underbelly and because she acted so much like Susie. We could see the hunting instinct in her as she stalked squirrels and other critters, and, just as Susie had done, she ran like the wind. Beyond that, her lineage was a wild guess. There was some collie, and the vet thought she was also part mountain dog, of sorts. She had a double coat. A second coat of short, tan fur lay beneath the long, white outer coat. Our climate was too hot for her, and she constantly shed the white fur, year round. What a mess. When I walked outside, little puffs of white fur would float past me. The air carried the downy stuff far and wide, and I found it stuck in shrubs everywhere. Birds loved it, and we discovered a number of nests that were lined with Lily fur.

I dreamed of a dog vacuum that could have sucked off all the white stuff at one sitting. Fortunately, unlike Susie, Lily loved getting a bath. She would sit patiently for hours while she was being groomed, and she happily would have done this every day. She was a very affectionate animal. She was also intelligent. I never bothered to teach her anything, but she quickly learned "sit," "come," and other basic commands by watching Jasmine.

Lily had no bad habits, except that she developed a taste for the climbing rose I had planted to grow across the top of the picket fence. She patiently snacked around the thorns, which discouraged her from eating too much at a time. It wasn't much of a problem. The rose just acted like it had been pruned and soon sprouted more leaves for Lily to munch. Some of the flower buds managed to escape Lily's nibbling habit, and we actually had blooms. Lily did not like to eat wood, and I was very happy that Jasmine stopped the behavior after Lily arrived.

Jasmine and Lily remained inseparable companions until Jasmine grew old with silver hair sprinkled through her black fur. We all grieved the loss of another beloved pet when she died. We buried her under a weeping Japanese maple tree in the woodland garden, and a few years later we would lay Lily to rest beside her. A muscadine vine draped from an overhanging branch, and a wild black cherry tree dropped fruit near the grave. I thought Jasmine's doggie ghost would like that.

When Jasmine died, I was concerned that Lily might not adapt well to life without her best friend. Lily knew that Jasmine was gone. When I looked into her unhappy, questioning eyes, I could tell that she was grieving.

At the time, my parents' failing health had made it impossible for them to care for their own dog, a black chow chow mix named Rock. My mother was already living in a nursing home, and my dad had been in the hospital for several weeks after suffering a severe stroke. My brother George went by my parents' house regularly to feed Rock, but otherwise the dog was alone. When it became clear that my dad would never return to his house, my brothers and I discussed what to do. With Jasmine gone, Lou and I had the space and facilities for another dog. My home seemed the obvious choice. Maybe Rock would be a good companion to Lily.

But Rock was an old dog with health problems of his own. He had spent the first years of his life outdoors in all sorts of weather, attached to a chain in the back yard of my father's next door neighbor, a solitary man with few visitors. The man fed Rock but otherwise did not interact with him. Dad watched with disapproving eyes and befriended the dog when the neighbor wasn't looking. Then one day, without a word and apparently without making arrangements for the dog's care, the neighbor disappeared. Horrified that the man had abandoned his dog to perish, Dad began carrying food and water to the lonely animal. After more than a week had passed with no word from the neighbor, he removed the chain and brought Rock to his own home, where the dog had a spacious fenced-in yard in which to play and where both of my parents lavished him with love and attention.

Six weeks after he vanished, the neighbor reappeared without explanation. My dad never knew what had happened, but he speculated that the man had been in jail. The guy came over to see my father.

"Mr. Henderson," the neighbor said, "you know that is my watch dog."

"And I am telling you, Rock belongs to me now."

My dad added some other choice words, with threats to call the Humane Society to file a report of animal abuse. The man left without Rock and never said another word about it.

Lou was concerned that the early years of neglect may have had a negative impact on Rock. We didn't know what other breed contributed to Rock's genetic make-up, but chow chows don't have the best reputation regarding temperament. Lou worried that the dog could be dangerous. He did not seem dangerous to me, but he did seem lonely and unhappy. He was missing my dad. Rock had become my parents' beloved pet, and they always had bragged about his good qualities. After years of serving as their faithful watch dog, he deserved better than a trip to the executioner's office.

"We don't need another dog," Lou said firmly.

"Of course we don't need another dog. That's not the point," I argued. "The point is the dog needs another family."

Lou agreed to try it. As I drove to my parents' house, I wasn't sure what would happen. Rock had seen me over the years whenever I had come to visit, but he was not attached to me. Some of Lou's concerns flashed through my mind. Rock had rarely been on a leash. What if he had flashbacks to his years on a chain when I tried to attach a leash? What if he did not want to leave his spacious yard and comfortable dog house? What if he refused to get into my car? I prayed that all would go well. His life depended on it.

I opened the gate and called Rock to me. "Hey, big boy, are you ready to come live with me?" I petted him and slipped the leash onto his collar. "Come on. It's time to go."

Rock looked up at me with eyes as deep and dark as well water. He had thick, long, brownish-black fur. He looked like a baby bear. Years ago he must have been the most adorable puppy, ever.

"Come on." I walked toward the gate, pulling gently on the leash.

Rock looked at me again, then pushed past me and headed out of the yard, straight toward my van. When I opened the passenger door, he hopped in and did not look back.

Rock adjusted to our routines easily and demonstrated a gentle and humble nature. He had always been a man's dog, and soon he and Lou grew fond of each other.

"This is a good dog. I wish we'd had him since he was a puppy." Lou would say.

We brought Rock's doghouse from my parents' place. In contrast to the large modern igloo that Lily used, it resembled an old mountain cabin, with cedar clapboards, a green roof, and a front porch. We placed it in a corner of the dog yard about three feet from the picket fence. The climbing rose arched over that spot and draped across the doghouse's roof. Rock loved toys, and his hoard included an infant's squeaky hedgehog that had originally belonged to Sam, a couple of rubber bones, and an assortment of balls. He kept them all together between his house and the fence, under the shelter of the rose. It's was like a little cave in there, and Rock liked to lie inside his rose-covered bower with his stash of playthings nestled next to his body.

Rock was not the instant best friend to Lily that Jasmine had been, although the two did tolerate one another. Rock and Lily strolled side by side on their daily walks with me, and sometimes I would catch them playing together inside the dog yard. But most of the time they lay in separate corners, like a worn-out couple that had given up on conversation.

At first, Rock had one bad habit that clearly irritated Lily: he liked to put his dirty paws in the water bowl, muddying the fresh drinking water. It did not matter if he had his own drinking bowl. He would muddy both of them. Lily watched the uncouth old dog do this a few times, wondering at his stupidity, until finally she couldn't take it any longer. Determined to put a stop to this unsanitary practice, she approached him as he stood with his front paws in the drinking bowl and barked at him sternly, reprimanding him for his filthy behavior. Rock looked surprised, but he never did it again.

Rock lived with us about nine months. Then one morning, not long after my father himself had succumbed to complications of the stroke he had suffered, we found that Rock, sleeping under the rose bush with his collection of toys next to his body, had passed away quietly in the night.

Afterwards, Lily seemed content to being an only dog. She was a mature animal and did not mind entertaining herself. But I would gather some doggie treats a couple times a day and head for the dog yard, and Lily would wag her tail with enthusiasm when she greeted me.

"Ready to go for your walk? Sit!"

She would sit and wait for her treat. Then the two of us would set out to explore, always excited to see what we could find just around the next bend of the road.

CHAPTER TWELVE

ⒶUTUMN

I do not believe in reincarnation, not at all—but if I did, I would be wondering.

One day I was sitting in the five-foot wooden swing that hangs from a large arbor in the area that had once been the children's playground. The boys were grown now, off to college and careers. To ease the passing of the era, we had given the climbing tower, slides, and swings to another family whose children were still young, and I had developed a quiet garden space in the place where my boys' voices once echoed as they played. It was bittersweet. So many memories were tied to that play equipment. I called the new garden my arbor garden. It was verdant and mossy, with ferns and other woodland plants. Our pets were all gone, and I liked to get my animal fix by sitting in the swing, listening to and watching the abundant wildlife in the trees that bordered the area.

Barred owls nested in the woods nearby. These huge predatory birds have distinctive calls, and if one is not accustomed to them, their unearthly sounds can curdle one's blood. They are interesting creatures. One day I watched from the patio as a barred owl perched atop the arbor, about twenty feet away. The bird calmly sat for at least ten minutes as it surveyed the surrounding territory, perhaps searching for a meal. It repeatedly swiveled its head, 180 degrees front to back without moving its body, like the demon-possessed character in the movie, *The Exorcist*.

It was totally creepy.

Lou once had his own encounter with one of these big birds. He was walking near the arbor garden one day when he noticed a barred owl perched in a nearby tree. The bird was watching him. Lou noted the bird and then went about his business. He soon heard the flutter of wings and looked up to see that the owl had followed him. He walked a little farther along the path, and again the owl flew to a branch within feet of him. Lou looked at the owl. The owl gazed right back. Was Lou too close to a nest? Or was the owl simply curious, wondering about this strange human character?

Another time, a mother owl and her baby caught my attention as they perched in an oak tree on the far edge of the arbor garden. I sat quietly in the swing and watched. Mama began to encourage the youngster to fly. She flew from branch to branch, obviously calling for the little one to follow. Baby finally took off, following her on short hops at first, and then mama and baby soared together from one side of the arbor garden to the other, a distance of about forty feet. I felt like a proud godmother.

Today, I had plopped myself into the swing with plans to savor the afternoon with its shimmering fall colors. The year had progressed into November, and the air was as fresh and crisp as the gala apple I had just eaten with my lunch. Take a bite, and sweet-tart juice squirts out. I admired the colorful view of the wide, tree-lined path that led from the arbor garden to the more open, sunnier front lawn. Golden sunbeams filtered down through the treetops, illuminating the red-orange leaves and creating light and dark patterns on the path.

"Meow!"

A cat had mysteriously appeared on the trail, and the animal came running rapidly toward me, her tail hoisted in the air like a flag flying.

"Mee-oww! Mee-oww!"

I was surprised. I had never seen the cat before, but the cat acted like she had been searching for me her whole life and couldn't believe her good fortune.

"Mee-oww!" Without hesitation, the kitty hopped up onto the swing and began to purr loudly. She climbed into my lap and nuzzled me under my neck.

"Well, hello, cat. Who are you?" I eyed her as she began to knead my lap. "Hey, I am a stranger to you. You do not belong to me. Don't you know that?"

She purred even louder. I looked her over. She was gorgeous, with luxuriously long, silken, gray and white fur. She was well fed and healthy. She looked young but was close to adult size. She lovingly gazed up at me with golden-green eyes and then partially lowered her eyelids as she nuzzled me again, relishing the moment.

"Meow." She licked my hand.

For some reason, I began to think about my mother, who had passed away earlier in the year, just four months after my dad. Mom, the consummate animal lover, had jokingly told me she wanted to come back as a cat. My mother had been a beautiful woman when she was young. I looked at the lovely creature in my lap and had the oddest feeling. As I said, I do not believe in reincarnation.

"I am going to check out the garden. Want to come?"

I lifted the cat and then plopped her at my feet as I stood. She rubbed my ankles, and when I started down the path, she hurriedly followed after me.

Thus began my relationship with Garden, the cat who did not belong to me. I called her Garden, because she would come running every day as I walked through my yard. She attended me faithfully as I inspected plants and performed small chores. Garden watched and sometimes commented about what I was doing. I wondered if she kept a lookout for me, or did she have some instinctive sense of when I was out and about? I never knew her real name. Nor did I ever meet her owners, though I knew they took good care of her. Garden was a contented cat. She had bright eyes and shiny fur. After visiting with me, Garden would often head through the woods toward the neighboring subdivision, so I assumed that her home was over there.

Although Garden was an elegant cat, she had a mischievous streak. One day in March of the following year I decided to spread some pine straw in the garden. Pine straw is readily available in Alabama and is commonly used around plants as mulch. It inhibits weed growth and enriches the soil as it decomposes. I love how it neatens the planting areas. Fresh pine straw also has a sweet, sharp, refreshing smell that I find particularly pleasing. I was bent over with my head down as I spread the straw around some hydrangeas. A movement caught my eye, and I glanced up.

Garden was a few feet in front of the hydrangeas. Her belly was low, and she was slinking forward, her eyes intense as she stalked her prey. It was clear to see who was her intended victim: me. She halted when she realized that I was watching her.

"What are you doing?" I asked. "Playing tiger in the wild?"

Her eyes narrowed for a moment as her body tensed. Then she pounced.

I thought she was going to land on my head, but she dove headfirst into the pine straw in front of me, where she buried all of her body except for her rear end and tail. She rolled over and over, kicking pine straw in all directions in a most unlady-like way, until she finally landed on her feet.

I laughed. "You are certainly frisky today!" I knew just how Garden felt. Spring does that to you. The gusto of the new season affected us all—humans, birds and bees, dogs and cats, and myriads of other creatures.

My feline friend came up to me, purring enthusiastically. I spent a few minutes petting her and picking pine straw out of her fur as we sat together on a nearby concrete bench.

Garden expected that bench visit. It was part of our routine. One day our walk was shorter than usual. My friend stayed by my side until we reached the walkway that led to the front door. Then she did a strange thing. She leaped in front of me, then turned and firmly batted my legs—no claws were involved, just the soft pads of her feet. Every time I took a step forward, she batted me. She was telling me that she was not ready for our walk to end. So we strolled about a bit more, and we sat on the concrete bench, and we discussed important world affairs. Finally, she hopped down and headed back toward her own house. She was holding her tail high, the sign of a happy cat.

With Garden, the cat who did not belong to me, I had the pleasures of pet ownership without any of the responsibilities. But several years after I met her, her visits stopped. I learned that some people in her neighborhood had moved, so I thought that must have been her family. I missed her, but I told myself that she was loved and had a good life.

Lou and I remained busy. I had returned to full-time work at the hospital. Lou was adamant—and I verbally agreed with him—that our pet-care days were over, except for some elderly fish that lingered on in our thirty-gallon tank. Life was easier without a pet. We could come and go on trips without the hassle of boarding animals or finding caregivers for them while we were gone. We did not have to buy pet food or spend money on expensive veterinary care. We did not have to play with them or make sure they were emotionally well adapted. We did not have to solve problems of bad behavior or annoying habits. And most of all, we did not have to suffer the wrenching pain of watching them die.

But...sometimes I felt a longing for a little body to love and care for. I could easily understand why people without children sometimes pour their emotional energy and resources into animals.

Then one autumn day, a tabby cat showed up in the yard. Her fur was short, gray and white striped with streaks of orange. She had lovely golden-green eyes, but I admit she looked much like many other tabby cats. At first glance she did not appear to be anything special.

She liked our vast yard with its infinite supply of voles and chipmunks, and she began to hang around. This was no pitiful, starving animal begging for shelter. While she was surely a stray and not a feral cat, this was a grown, fully confident mouser. She climbed in and out of trees with easy agility. Sometimes she surprised me as I walked in the garden. She would suddenly appear before me, sitting at eye-level and peering out at me from a leafy perch in a nearby tree. She had an extraordinary cat personality and an incredible connection to human language.

I admit to a tendency to anthropomorphize animals, assigning human traits and feelings to their behaviors and vocalizations. I like to talk to animals, and I often imagine what they would say if they could talk back (I think I am fairly accurate). I did not fully realize what a habit this was until one day when I was helping my friend Sue to plant flowers in her garden. I was babbling away as I dug a hole. I glanced up and saw her looking oddly at me.

"Oh, I'm sorry." I laughed. "I know I sometimes talk to myself."

Sue stared back. "And you also talk to worms."

But this cat genuinely seemed to carry on full conversations with me. She would listen to me, then answer with a string of meows, her voice rising and falling, the pauses and the changing pitch and intensity of her voice exactly echoing a person's speech pattern.

One day I watched her attempt to catch a bird that was hopping around under a shrub. She quietly slinked forward, eyeing her prey, and then pounced beneath the bush. I was rooting for the bird, and I was glad when it easily escaped.

The cat was not happy. She came out from under the shrub and shook her head, clearly disgusted.

"Meow!!" I am certain it was the feline version of a cuss word.

This kitty was not like Garden, who obviously loved and adored me, but she was friendly. She purred readily and allowed me to pet her. Lou warily watched my interaction with the stray cat.

"Don't feed that animal. We don't need another pet."

"I am not feeding her. She provides for herself just fine. She likes to eat ground squirrels."

Long ago I had openly admired ground squirrels (AKA chipmunks). Their fat cheeks, which contain handy storage pouches, round out like overloaded grocery sacks when they stuff their mouths with seeds and nuts, and they are among the cutest rodents on earth. Unfortunately, we created a world-class chipmunk problem when we installed several bird feeders, one next to the patio and a couple in front of the big windows across the front of the house.

I enjoyed watching an assortment of birds that regularly visited the feeders. I spent several weeks recovering from surgery one year, resting on the couch and watching the activity outside the windows. I kept a list of all the different types of birds that I saw come through the area. The list ended up with over thirty species.

Big gray squirrels liked the birdseed also, and they knocked the mixture all over the ground when they came to the feeders. The chipmunks came to gather the seed from the ground, and sometimes they ventured into the feeders themselves. They began to build their subterranean tunnels and burrows directly beneath the feeders. A huge underground chipmunk metropolis eventually spread far into the yard, with multiple entrance and exit holes. Clearly, a chipmunk land agent was out there, successfully promoting the amenities of the area.

I hoped that Lou would develop good thoughts about the stray cat if he knew she could help solve the chipmunk problem. I don't know if he himself had ever interacted with the cat. I had never seen him speak to her, but the animal was certainly aware of Lou. She had been hanging around for a couple of weeks when one morning she appeared in front of Lou as he exited the house onto the carport. A large dead rat was hanging from her mouth.

The cat plopped the rat at Lou's feet. Maybe she had heard that the way to a man's heart was through his stomach. She had carefully prepared it for him. The head was missing—it had been severed from the body of the rat as neatly as if it had been removed with a surgical knife. All traces of blood had been cleaned away.

"Lou, she has brought a present for you. This means that she likes you." I wanted to put a positive spin on the situation.

Lou gaped at the homeless cat and the gift she had presented to him. He did not say anything at first. Then he shook his head. "Cat, I don't need a rat. We don't have problems with rats. If you want to get into my good graces, you have to bring me a ground squirrel."

"Meow."

Later that day, Lou was out at the large woodpile behind the parking area chopping wood. We burn plenty of wood through the winter, and my husband likes to swing an ax and feel the wood split beneath the force of his blows. No doubt this reinforces his sense of masculine prowess. Fortunately, with our sizeable, tree-studded property, there is always wood that needs chopping. Winter was approaching, so Lou was working hard to split a good supply of logs, making sure they were just the right size for our large living room fireplace.

He looked up to see the stray cat hurrying toward the woodpile. Something was dangling from her mouth.

"What in the world…?"

The cat came to him and dropped a dead ground squirrel at his feet.

"Lou," I said when he told me what had happened, "what more can she do? We have to adopt her now."

And Lou agreed.

We named her Autumn, because that was the season of the year when she came to us. We took her to the vet to get her shots and to have her spayed. Afterwards, the vet was apologetic. Although she had not seen a scar from previous surgery, during the operation she discovered that Autumn had already been spayed.

To compensate for the needless surgery, the vet implanted an identification microchip. This involved injecting a tiny microchip, about the size of a piece of rice, under her skin between the shoulder blades. The microchip contained a registration number and a phone number for the registry. In the case that Autumn should wander away, this identification technology would allow a vet or animal shelter to use a hand held scanner to read information from the microchip. They would then be able to call the registry to find out our name and phone number in order to reunite us with our lost pet. Because Autumn had come to us as a stray, we appreciated the technology.

Autumn was always affectionate toward me, and we had many interesting conversations. But she clearly loved Lou best. She followed him around the property like a faithful puppy, her expressive eyes full of adulation. I was a bit miffed. But she had chosen her person, however undeserved, for her own reasons.

And Lou? One day he picked her up, and as she purred contentedly in his arms, he announced, "This is my cat."

Autumn loved the outdoors. She would stalk her target like a lioness creeping through the jungle, moving silently and with her sharp eyes sweeping the territory. We began to feed her nutritious, good quality cat food, and she enjoyed it. But she continued to catch and eat wild critters, especially voles.

Sometimes called field mice, voles are small rodents that are related to hamsters. I have been at war with them for many years. They are worse than ground squirrels. They like to burrow beneath plants and eat their succulent root systems. A large vole infestation can be extremely destructive to a garden. My mother gave me a small but exquisite weeping Japanese maple not long before she passed away. I put it in the arbor garden, and one day I sat in the swing and admired the young plant's colorful red leaves and weeping habit. It was growing well. The next morning I wandered down to the area and discovered that the Japanese maple had wilted overnight. Puzzled, I pulled at its stems, and the entire tree came out of the ground. The root system had been completely eaten away. Voles!

If Autumn caught a vole (and she was extremely good at catching voles), there was no hope for the animal. A vole was a delicacy to Autumn, and she would swallow the tasty meal within seconds. It didn't matter if we had just fed Autumn and her belly was bulging. That vole was a goner.

Chipmunks had a chance. Unless she was truly hungry, Autumn preferred to play with chipmunks. She would eye a chipmunk hole and crouch near it, patiently waiting for an unsuspecting victim to exit, whereupon she immediately pounced on the creature, gripping it between her front paws. Then she would carefully carry it in her mouth to a spot ten to fifteen feet away before dropping it. The unfortunate animal would usually lie there stunned for a few moments. Autumn would watch it and maybe give it a pat or two. Finally, the chipmunk would recover enough to make a run for it. Autumn would dash after it and repeat the catch and release maneuver. She would do this multiple times, until either the chipmunk died or managed to escape into a chipmunk tunnel, which did not upset her too much. If it died, she usually ate it. There was no point in wasting good meat.

Autumn's habit of "toying" with her prey was not intentional cruelty, as it might seem from human perspective, but natural instinct. Small creatures can have vicious bites, and this is one way cats protect themselves while hunting. If an animal is exhausted, it is less likely to put up resistance when the meal actually begins.

After we adopted Autumn, we removed our bird feeders. We also put a small, tinkling bell on Autumn's collar. We did not want to present our cat with easy bird targets. We were happy that Autumn preferred going after voles and chipmunks. I never saw her catch a bird, so I think that they generally were safe from her.

Our upstairs sitting area, accessible from the back hallway, became Autumn's domain. Lou placed a blanket on a couch up there, and this was her favorite spot when she wasn't curled up in Lou's lap. I had put some of the boys' old toys on a low shelf near the couch, including a basket of beanie babies. Beanie babies are small stuffed toys filled with little plastic pellets. They were quite popular when my children were young, and some became expensive collector items. One afternoon as I walked toward Lou's office at the back of the house, a beanie baby came tumbling down the stairs. Then another one, and another. I looked up the stairs. Autumn was at the top, the next beanie baby in mouth. She dropped it onto the floor and batted it down to me.

Afterwards, I purchased a number of cat toys, but our cat turned her nose up at most of them. Like a small child who plays with the box rather than the gift it contains, she preferred to choose her own play objects. The exception was a laser pointer thing that I used to shine a dot on the floor or wall, moving it up and down, back and forth, and around in circles. Autumn never grew tired of playing tag with it. She would run and leap at the little dot of light until she fell over, temporarily exhausted, but soon she would be up and game for more.

Autumn settled well into our household. When our boys came home to visit, they were all impressed with our special cat.

But a year after we adopted her, Autumn disappeared. None of the neighbors had seen her. There was no little body lying in the road. I searched the woods and drove around all the neighboring subdivisions, hoping to find her. Nothing. Weeks, months passed. We sometimes had seen coyotes in the area, and Lou thought that probably one of them had caught our cat. Autumn was gone.

Lou did not say much, but I knew this must have hurt him. We removed all the cat toys and gave away the cat food, kitty litter, and other cat supplies.

A full year after she disappeared, I received a call from a veterinarian.

"We have your cat."

"What!" I was dumbfounded. "She has been gone a year!"

A woman had found Autumn wandering a few miles from our house, on the far side of the lake at Joe Tucker Park. She explained that the cat had come up to her, meowing pitifully, and she recognized that the cat was lost. She was not wearing a collar, but she did appear well fed and healthy. The good lady had carried her to a local vet, who scanned her for a microchip and then came up with our information.

I could tell the vet was smiling on the other end of the telephone. "Well, we have her now, and I'm sure she would like to come home."

"OK, that's great! I'm on my way!"

I could hardly believe it.

"Lou! Lou! Someone found Autumn!" Lou was working in his office, and I hurried to give him the news. "I'm going to get her now. Wow! After a year, I hope she remembers us."

I was excited but also concerned. How would she react to us? Where had she been all this time? Had she been adopted (stolen!) by yet another owner, who now would be missing her?

When the vet brought Autumn out to me, she came into my arms without hesitation, but she did not meow or purr. Her silence bothered me. What was she thinking? I put her in the car and headed for home. When I tried to talk to her, she had little reaction, but sat watching out the passenger side window. Then, when I turned onto our drive, she suddenly became very alert, raising her head and opening her eyes wide to take in the scenery. As we approached the house, she put her front paws on the window and pulled herself up to better see. She began to purr vigorously. She looked at me.

"Meow!"

I parked in the carport and opened the car door. Autumn hopped out and headed straight for the back door.

We entered the house, and there was Lou, waiting with arms open wide.

"Meee-oow."

This time Autumn was home to stay.

EPILOGUE

Time moves fast, rolling over itself with increasing speed with the passage of each year. Helena continues to grow, now with over 20,000 inhabitants and sprouting subdivisions like mushrooms in the rainy season. There are also plans to build a new town center and a sports and leisure complex. However, Helena maintains its small town appeal. It was a great place to raise my children and continues to be a family-centered community.

Sometimes visiting youngsters open a trunk filled with my children's old toys, and recollections of the sounds and antics of small boys cavorting through the house come spilling out along with the playthings. Other memories are put away in the crevices of my home and whisper to me as I pass. I occasionally take them out of a box or down from a shelf to visit for a while.

I am glad my sons grew up in this place with a menagerie of animals and surrounded by nature. A young boy, age five, visited us a while back with his father. The man was a single parent, and he was doing his best to raise his son alone. The child spent his days in preschool and daycare, and most of his evenings were spent in front of the television inside their small apartment. I looked forward to his visit. I was eager to introduce him to our yard and to explore its paths with him. But, sadly, the child would have none of it. He stood out front, looked over the spacious lawn and the woodlands surrounding it, and then demanded he be allowed to go back inside and watch television.

"But why?" I asked. "There is so much to see and do out here."

He shook his head firmly. "It's too big."

I wonder how many children today know little or nothing about nature, who have never had a chance to dig in the dirt or to explore the woods with their dogs. How can we expect to save the environment if we don't teach our children to respect and care for it and to understand how all the myriads of creatures are part of the whole plan, designed to work together? How can a human being learn these things from video games or violent movies?

My boys are grown men now, and it is a challenge to get everyone together at the same time. Mark lives in California's Silicon Valley, working as an engineer with a start-up company, which could end up making him either very rich or very poor. Josh in his younger days thought about making music his career—he was an excellent jazz guitarist—but ultimately he decided that music was more fun as a hobby. Instead, he became a web developer, and he enjoys freedom to work from anywhere. He lived in Oregon for over a decade, and since then he has spent years traveling in Southeast Asia, an area of the world that always fascinated him, as well as other parts of the globe.

Sam remains in Alabama. He works as a computer software consultant. He has maintained a love of nature, including both domesticated and wild animals, and he has inherited a bit of the gardening bug from me. He likes to come over to inspect my plants and to offer suggestions about natural soil amendments and organic pesticides.

Both Sam and Mark have done well managing their diabetes, and neither, except for Sam's initial hospitalization, has been hospitalized because of the disease. Modern technology has made diabetes care easier, with blood glucose monitoring systems that do not involve finger pricks and pumps that will infuse insulin without needle injections. But it remains a disease that requires careful control, and it can be deadly if ignored.

As for Lou and myself, we are now retired. But not tired! We remain very busy.

Lou has always loved camping, hiking, and other scouting type adventures. He enjoys teaching boys and young men about those activities and for years has been involved with a church group that promotes physical, mental, and spiritual development through outdoor pursuits. An important lesson the students soon learn is that if it rains (and it will, especially if there has been at a drought of at least six weeks), if it freezes (no problem, you get a special badge for that!), or if the temperature is ninety-five degrees Fahrenheit and the thick, humid air feels exactly like a steam room, you go camping anyway—you will learn something about yourself and you will have a great time.

We both enjoy working in our garden, which now spreads out over most of our large property. People sometimes are intimidated by its size and wonder how we managed to do all this. I remind them that it did not happen overnight. I tell them it was birthed a long time ago, on February 10, 1990, the night that a tornado destroyed the center of our property and forced me into serious gardening. I realized through that long recovery process that I loved the creativity of garden design and that I relished the physical labor that comes with planting and maintenance. It is a lot of work, or play, depending on one's definitions.

A few years ago I took a Master Gardener course, complete with an almost two-inch thick textbook and weekly tests. I felt like I was back in college! (However, true confession: a great deal, if not most, of what I know about growing plants has come from other gardeners, as well as the very hard master of trial and error. But it's good to have that giant reference book when I need it.) Now I am a Certified Master Gardener, and public education is an important part of our mandate. I enjoy talking to garden clubs and other groups, teaching them about growing plants and sharing my gardening experiences. I also published a successful garden blog, *Deb's Garden*, for over ten years. My blog connected me to other garden lovers, and, tucked away as we are in a hidden corner of Helena, it allowed me to share my garden with the world. The blog expanded my horizons and made me a better gardener.

As I stroll through the garden or walk through my home, I may note a place, a plant, or an object that reminds me of the many animals that inhabited our lives and rounded out our days, who educated us and entertained us and often amazed us, and who became an important part of our family's history.

I smile when I pass the big stone planter across the front of the house, remembering Susie and the War of the Planter. Junipers still grow in that planter. Looking out the kitchen window, I think about Sam and Shepherd—only yesterday, it seems—coming up out of the valley together, bringing some creature they have captured.

So many memories: a lizard named Spot-Spike; Whiskers who taught me about being a squirrel mama; sweet, intelligent, soccer-playing Jasmine and her best friend Lily, whose fluffy white fur was a favorite bird-nesting material. There was humble Rock, my dad's old dog—after Rock was gone, we fancified his dog house with turquoise paint on the clapboards and a red roof, and it became a decorative element in our garden. And I will never forget Miss Pepper bouncing around the patio with a knotted towel in her mouth, enticing me to play tug-of-war, or Autumn, our amazing cat, batting beanie babies down the back stairs.

But life moves on. We don't have any pets today, but who can say what tomorrow may bring? Meanwhile, I still thrill at the sight of a box turtle, a rabbit, a dragonfly, or a butterfly. Squirrels scamper through the trees, and birds fill the woodlands with their songs. And once in a while I am permitted to briefly cross the barrier that naturally separates humans from wildlife.

Recently I sat in the arbor swing and had a conversation with a juvenile barred owl, which was out of the nest but definitely not full grown. The bird was curious, and it began making cute little hoots at me from its perch about twenty feet away.

"Well, hello, little one. Where is your mama?"

The owl considered my question and hooted again.

"Does your mama know you're talking to a strange human?"

"Hoo. Hoo." The bird was looking directly at me. Then, growing bolder, the young owl flew closer and landed about ten feet away.

"Are you lonely?"

"Hoo. Hoo."

"Well, I'm glad to make your acquaintance."

"Hoo. Hoo."

This amazing encounter went on for at least five minutes, until a larger owl showed up and said something to the youngster, who gave one more hoot in my direction, then flew away with its parent.

Each day of life is full of promise. I will forever cherish the past, and I think about and plan for tomorrow. But most important are the todays with all the small moments that eventually flow together to create an era. Scripture says, and I have seen the truth of it through life with my family, including all my critters:

"This is the day that the Lord has made. Let us rejoice and be glad in it."

THE END

$\mathcal{A}$CKNOWLEDGEMENTS

Above all, I give thanks to God—to my Heavenly Father who gave me all the gifts of this life, to His Son Jesus whose death and resurrection promise me far greater gifts yet to come, and to His Spirit who strengthened me and guided me all along the way. To God be the glory!

To my very talented friend, Ron Adair, whose beautiful illustrations add so much to *Family Tails*: Thank you, Ron, for the hours and hours you spent working on these illustrations, laboring to make sure every detail was exactly right. Thank you for believing that my book was worthy of your time and efforts, and thank you for your patience with me! And thanks to your wife Beth, who first brought *Family Tails* to your attention!

To Ray-Lynn Snowden, my good friend from high school, with whom I reconnected after 50 years at our Banks High 50th Year Reunion: Who would believe that after all those years we still would have so much in common, though different things than when we were teens. Now we share a mutual love of gardening, nature, animals (especially English Setters!), the art of writing and wordsmithing, and a long-standing admiration for the Alabama Crimson Tide football team!

Without your initial encouragement and support I probably would never have published *Family Tails* for the public, as it was originally meant to be just for my family. Thank you for the many days you spent poring over pages, proofreading and editing. Thank you for pushing me to make Family Tails the best that it can be.

Though we live in different states, I always look forward to our delightful phone conversations. I am forever grateful for our long-distance but close friendship.

I owe special thanks to college professor and award-winning author, Brad Strickland: Your insight, advice, and encouragement meant so much. You were a complete stranger to me, and your willingness to read *Family Tails* and to give your honest opinion was instrumental in my decision to go public with my book. Thank you also for your very valuable manuscript overview.

Thanks also to book designer and formatter, Ghislain Viau: You took all those files and turned them into a beautiful book! I am impressed with your technical skills and creative flair. Thank you for answering my many questions. I am especially grateful for all the technical advice and help that you gave.

To Brian Puckett, Mayor of Helena, Alabama, to Karen Snowden, and to Jenny Wheeler: I appreciate your taking time out of your overloaded schedules to read this book and to write reviews. A very big thanks to you all!

To all my neighbors and friends who encouraged me in this endeavor: You each have been a special blessing to me, and some of you will find yourselves in this book. I promise I did not say anything bad about anybody!

And to my family who have loved me and allowed me to put our story into print: Of course, this is all for you. Thank you for the memories! I love you dearly.

$\mathcal{A}$UTHOR PROFILE

Deborah Elliott is a wife, mother, nurse, teacher, and writer. She is a long-time resident of Helena, Alabama, where she and her husband Louis raised three boys and their menagerie of pets. She is a graduate of the University of Alabama in Birmingham and has worked as a nurse and as a community educator. Her memoir, *Family Tails: My Life With Boys, Dogs, and Other Amazing Critters*, is her first book.